The Russian Winter, the American Fall, The Chinese Spring—and Summer

The Russian Winter, The American Fall, The Chinese Spring —and Summer

A Historian's Fairy Tale

Edited by
Leonard R. Friedman, M.D., J.D.

VANTAGE PRESS
New York   Washington   Atlanta   Hollywood

FIRST EDITION

Copyright © 1979 by Leonard R. Friedman, M.D., J.D.

Published by Vantage Press, Inc.
516 West 34th Street, New York, New York 10001

Manufactured in the United States of America
Standard Book Number 533-02957-0

Dedicated to those who provide inspiration:

Thomas Atkins
Richard Coppedge
Edward Daniels
Lon Fuller
Llewelyn Legters
Edgar Snow
Alan Studner
—and my wife

TABLE OF CONTENTS

PREFACE
THE FAIRY TALE

This collection of papers, written during the 1960s, was compiled by a client in psychotherapy. It is a historian's notebook, concerned with the politics of the superpowers, and the quest for appropriate authority figures in the twentieth century. Through psychotherapy the client has overcome his reticence to release these papers, provided they would not be released for a period of not less than four years after his therapy ended.

The client had no degree in either history or the social sciences, but he stated that he was once told by Joel Kupperman (a former "Quiz Kid") that, next to Joel, he knew more about nothings (facts) than anyone other than Joel himself. From being a collector of facts, the client progressed to placing these facts in a perspective which is unique and does not appear to try to follow any school of historical thought.

The client's story has always been fascinating. He remembered predicting in 1960 the exact number of votes John F. Kennedy would receive on the first ballot of the Democratic Nominating Convention, as well as the exact number of electoral votes which President Kennedy received in the national election. He based his findings on the shift of Catholic votes back to the Democratic party during that election year.

In 1961 an elderly Chinese physician asked the client to read *The Conquerors* by André Malraux. The physician told the client the book described a significant period of Chinese history through which the physician had lived. The figure of Vasily Bleucher, the book's hero, became an object of intense interest. The client's final feelings were that Vasily Bleucher was a pseudonym for a Jewish Soviet marshal named Stern who had served under various pseudonyms in the Ukraine, the Urals, Siberia, and China. Serving in Spain, Bleucher or Stern was known as General Klèber, commander of the International Brigade in Madrid. From his expanding knowledge of Vasily Bleucher, the client was able to unravel the mystery of succession in both the Soviet Union and China, as the unpublished letters to the editors of the *New York Times* reveal.

As the client's grasp of theories of history became more sophisticated, he turned to a study of the American Civil War. From the client's research into the Civil War, Union Major General George Henry Thomas, a Virginian, emerged as pivotal to the understanding of American national interest. By applying the Bleucher formula, that of the military-political figure who, behind the scene, taught and influenced the lives of later significant figures, another fascinating individual had appeared. To the client, General Thomas thus provided the crucial link in maintaining continuity from the decades prior to the Civil War through the present time. As Commander of the XIVth Corps and later as Commander of the Army of the Cumberland, General Thomas had as his subordinates General James Garfield as Chief of Staff, General Andrew Jackson as political advisor, and General Benjamin Harrison as division commander. Other political dynasties, such as the Palmers of Illinois and the Coxes of Ohio, were also founded by their links to General Thomas.

Later, while meditating on the nature of real army life, the client had an opportunity to study American history from 1898 to the present. His studies were directed toward such questions as why we were in Vietnam and what the United States could offer in an advisory capacity during wars of national liberation.

When, from 1966 to 1969, the Red Guards were unleashed in China, the client returned to theorizing about China and the meaning of Mao's Red Guards. Later at the end of a decade of anxiety, some of the client's solutions to the problems of our times emerged. The articles which come in the part called "Summer" are suggestions for a United Nations Peacekeeping Force, for restructuring the United States Army, and for understanding Mao Tse-tung as a significant lawgiver in our time. The book's title, *The Russian Winter, the American Fall, the Chinese Spring—and Summer*, best synopsizes the attitude of the client toward understanding the superpowers in the seventies.

The client considered the life of a historian to be a lonely one, a world which consists of stringing together facts with a succession of ideas. He felt that one who deals with nothings is outwardly rewarded with commensurate value, yet earns an internal satisfaction unmatched by other fields. He appreciated his wife's understanding and patience during the years he was spinning his tales of history, which she perhaps perceived as the ramblings of a hyper individual. Of course, his relationship with his father had a great deal to do with his perseverance in writing the studies, in his search for appropriate authority figures.

The client would like to express his appreciation to my secretaries who, over the years, have typed and revised the manuscripts. They are Anne Robinson and Linda Axelrod. The client himself has not received recognition or reward for his work. He would prefer the anonymity shared by his heroes in history. I respect that feeling and hope the reader indulges the client in his desire. Another desire is for the royalties of his book to be set in trust for the establishment of a Peace Academy, devoted to studying the world's follies and presenting solutions to these problems.

The Russian Winter, the American Fall,
The Chinese Spring—and Summer

PART I. / THE RUSSIAN WINTER

INTRODUCTION

The unpublished letters speak for themselves. The first letter, written during the Cuban Missile Crisis in 1962, suggested that Leonid Brezhnev and Aleksei Kosygin were Nikita Khrushchev's opposition in the Soviet Union. Six months later, in response to a *New York Times Magazine* article, it was suggested that Brezhnev and Kosygin would succeed Khrushchev and that Lin Piao was heir apparent to Mao Tse-tung. These letters summarized the conclusions reached after writing an unpublished manuscript entitled "The Riddle of Soviet Power: An Answer to an Enigma." In essence, the riddle of succession in both the Soviet Union and China had been solved. The 1961 manuscript was followed by an article on the role of the KGB in Soviet power politics and one on the chilling effects of the Soviet invasion of Czechoslovakia entitled "Why Khrushchev Remembers." The 1968 attempt on the life of Leonid Brezhnev and the subsequent demise of more than 100 Soviet generals led to the feeling that, once again, an icy glacier had stretched over the Russian lands.

DRAMATIS PERSONAE

The Players (in some order of importance)

Vasily Konstantinovich Bleucher, Marshal of the Soviet Union—
Also known as: Stern, Galen, Sternberg, Klèber (1889–1938)
[Gebhard Leberecht Blücher, Prussian Marshal (1742–1819)]
[Jean Baptiste Klèber, French Revolutionary General (1753–
1800)]

Ivan Stepanovich Konev, Marshal of the Soviet Union (1897–
1973)

Rodion Yakovevich Malinovsky, Marshal of the Soviet Union
(1889–1967)

Konstantin Konstantinovich Rokossovsky, Marshal of the Soviet
Union (1896–1968)

Vasily Ivanovich Chuikov, Marshal of the Soviet Union (1900–)

Kliment Efremovich Voroshilov, Marshal of the Soviet Union
(1881–1969)

Georgi Konstantinovich Zhukov, Marshal of the Soviet Union
(1895–)

Leonid Ilich Brezhnev, First Secretary of the Communist Party
(1906–)

Aleksei Nikolaevich Kosygin, Premier of the Soviet Union
(1904–)

Nikita Sergeevich Khrushchev, First Secretary of the Communist
Party (1894–1971)

Joseph Stalin (Iosif Vissarionovich Dzhugashvili) First Secretary of
the Communist Party (1879–1953)

Georgi Maximilianovich Malenkov, Premier of the Soviet Union
(1902–1975)

Vyacheslav Mikailovich Molotov, member of the Politburo
(1890–)

Trotsky (Leo Davydovich Bronstein), Bolshevik leader (1877–
1940)

Laurenti Pavlovich Beria, Chief of Public Security (1899–1953)

Demetri Stepanovich Polyanski, member of the Politburo
(1917–)

Demetri Fetorovich Ustinov, member of the Politburo (1908–)

KEY ACTS

Russo-Japanese War	1904–5
First Russian Revolution	1905
Kerensky Premier, end of Romanov Dynasty	July, 1917
Lenin and the Bolsheviks to power	November, 1917
Treaty of Versailles	June, 1919
League of Nations	1920–46
Stalin to power	1924–25
Bleucher to Canton and China	1924–27
Japanese Invasion of Manchuria	1931
Spanish Civil War	July, 1936–39
Siege of Madrid	October, 1936–39
Japanese-Soviet War in Outer Mongolia	September, 1939
Soviet-German Invasion of Poland—World War II	September 1, 1939
Soviet Russia at war with Finland	November, 1939–March, 1940
German Invasion of the Soviet Union	June 22, 1941
Soviet Counteroffensive at Moscow	December 6, 1941
Soviet Counteroffensive at Stalingrad	November, 1942
D-Day, Invasion of France	June 6, 1944
Atomic bombs on Japan	August 6, 9, 1945
Soviet Invasion of Manchuria	August 8, 1945
VJ Day	September 2, 1945
Death of Joseph Stalin	March, 1953
Malenkov to power	1953
Dismissal of Laurenti P. Beria	July, 1953
Beria dies	Autumn, 1953
Wladyslaw Gomulka to power in Poland	October, 1956
Hungarian Revolt	October, 1956
Cuban Missile Crisis	October 22–28, 1962
Khrushchev removed from power	October 14, 1964
Soviet Invasion of Czechoslovakia	August 20, 1968

SECTION I / UNPUBLISHED LETTERS

(BY THE CLIENT)

Letter to the Editor
New York Times
New York

November 10, 1962

Dear Sir:

As an observer of the Soviet scene I would register objections to any reference to Marshal Rodion Y. Malinovsky as a so-called Stalinist. Stalinism or any totalitarianism represents the aggressive misuse of millions of individuals for the personal gain and for the selfish ambition of a handful of men. The life and philosophy of Malinovsky point to a man more interested in Russia and its individuals than in personal gain.

Malinovsky's service to the Russian people began in 1920 in Siberia where he instructed the Siberian nationalities in the use of the more modern weapons of war for their defense against outside domination. During the Russian Civil War the armed Siberians were to defeat in turn the Cossacks who represented the instruments of the former tsarist oppression and the Japanese who were attempting to annex Siberian territory. Malinovsky's talents were then added to those of Vasily Bleucher, Ivan Konev, and Konstantin Rokossovsky to build the unbeatable elite Siberian Armies of the Soviet military. These Siberian Army officers have constantly stressed in their building of a military force a people's army for defensive wars. They have taught that any offensive action would ultimately lead to defeat. Malinovsky was to lead the Siberian Armies in part and then as overall commander from 1920 to 1955. The Siberian Armies were used effectively on the eve of World War II to crush Japanese encroachments in Soviet Russia and in Outer Mongolia. These armies were then to provide the 1,000,000 man reserve that Georgi Zhukov and Stalin were to unleash on December 7, 1941, to unhinge and roll back the German blitzkrieg. Rokossovsky, Konev and Malinovsky were personally to lead their men against the Germans from Moscow to Stalingrad, to Berlin, Prague, and Vienna. These brother officers have also stressed and contributed to the economic development of the then underdeveloped Asiatic Russia. During the thirties, Aleksei N. Kosygin was utilized to plan and to begin the industrialization of Siberia. This planning laid the groundwork for the giant industrial complex from the Urals to the Pacific which was to support the successful Soviet war effort. Later under Leonid Brezhnev, a former political commissar attached to the Siberian Armies, the agricultural development of Siberia was increased under the Siberian Virgin Lands Program of 1955. Interestingly enough, both projects under the direction of Khrushchev appointees have since bogged down in an administrative morass.

Malinovsky's stature in Russia rests on his successful defense of Russian territory and on the help he gave in modernizing Siberian industries and agriculture. This type of man, who has invested his life in building and defending Russia, is unlikely to be interested in burying this land in a nuclear holocaust. *Newsweek Magazine* of November 12, 1962, correctly ascribed the Soviet missile adventure in Cuba to the ambitions of Nikita Khrushchev. Malinovsky's reaction has been to moderate Khrushchev's influence on the Soviet Military by removing Marshal Maslenniko, a Khrushchev supporter. He has replaced this former head of the Rocket Troops with Marshal Sergei S. Biryuzov, who had formerly been Malinovsky's Chief of Staff within the Army. In the past certain commentators have looked at Zhukov and later at Khrushchev as our best friends in the Kremlin. Historically it will probably be clear that actually Malinovsky had been the moderating force on the ambitions of Zhukov and Khrushchev that has prevented a nuclear holocaust in the world. In a possible showdown between Malinovsky and Khrushchev, it would seem that Malinovsky, Brezhnev, and Kosygin are a better choice for

American support than the ambitious and unpredictable Nikita Khrushchev.

Sincerely,

Excerpt from Sunday Supplement, *New York Times*, April 28, 1963; pages 10-11:

AFTER KHRUSHCHEV? The secrecy which shrouds the activities of the Soviet leadership makes predictions about a possible successor to Khrushchev extremely speculative. A widely held view here is that the disappearance of Khrushchev from the political scene would be followed by the assumption of power by a triumvirate which would divide Khrushchev's duties and responsibilities. The triumvirate would consist of Frol R. Kozlov, 54, Leonid I. Brezhnev, 56, and Aleksei N. Kosygin, 59, with Kozlov the dominant personality as First Secretary of the Party.

Kozlov, a First Deputy Premier, now apparently ranks next to Khrushchev also in the party secretariat. He is a blunt, rather taciturn man who has risen through the ranks of the party and is regarded as a conservative organization man who is interested primarily in building a broad base of Soviet power through emphasis on heavy industry.

Brezhnev, now chairman of the Presidium of the Supreme Soviet and thus titular head of state, is a close associate of Khrushchev with a background of training in the party apparatus, industry, and agriculture. He is a man with considerable bearing and, in his present post, has had a good many contacts with foreigners and life abroad.

Kosygin, another First Deputy Premier, is a quiet man who has preferred to work in the background, concerned mainly with light industry and agriculture.

It is expected that the triumvirate would rule as leaders of the party presidium on a collective basis during a period of transition to a new power alignment.

—Seymour Topping.

AFTER MAO? If anything happens to Mao Tse-tung, the next leader of Communist China will be—barring some unforeseen development—Liu Shao-chi, present titular head of state. Liu, a lean, ascetic organizing genius, was more or less formally designated as Mao's heir apparent in 1959 when Mao relinquished the Chairmanship of the Republic to devote his entire energies to his other job as Chairman of the Chinese Communist Party Central Committee—which, in Mao's case, means he still remained the real ruler of Communist China. Liu, whose exact age is unknown, but is in the neighborhood of 62, give or take a couple of years, could be expected to outlive Mao, who is 69. However, Liu's health has been questionable for some time and this could affect his ascendency.

All observers agree that Chou En-lai, 65, the brilliant and personable Premier of the Republic and vice-chairman of the party's Central Committee, would be next in line after Liu as the top man in Red China. And after Chou? Here the line of succession is less clearly defined but, among a number of possible claimants, the most favored choice of China specialists is Teng Hsaio-p'ing, the short, dour Secretary General of the party. Teng, who is about 60, is a "dark horse" who was suddenly singled out for the honor of standing next to Mao in photographs made of the Central Committee's 10th plenary conference last September.

All three principal candidates to succeed Mao have been closely associated with the party chairman. It is unlikely that the accession of any one of them would bring a radical change in policy.

—Robert Trumbull

Letter to the Editor   28 April, 1963
New York Times
New York

Dear Sirs:

In your article "Most Likely to Succeed" of April 28, 1963, various personages were suggested as successors to Nikita Khrushchev and Mao Tse-tung. In an unpublished letter to the New York Times on November 10, 1962, I indicated that Leonid Brezhnev and Aleksei Kosygin were part of the opposition to Khrushchev in the Soviet Union. This letter was based on the assumption that their strength rested on their association with the military leaders then and still now entrenched in power in the Ministry of Defense in Moscow. The factor most overlooked by Kremlinologists is that it is the Soviet Marshals associated with the Soviet Siberian Armies and led by Rodion Y. Malinovsky who have achieved enough control of the Soviet scene to ease Khrushchev out gracefully.

Instead of the picture of Frol Kozlov, I would have placed a picture of Malinovsky. Kozlov certainly is Khrushchev's hand-picked successor as Khrushchev himself has indicated. However as Khrushchev is finally being appreciated as certainly not the most powerful man in the Soviet Union, this support is not enough to lead Kozlov to the post of First Secretary. In a vote for leadership Kozlov's support would be on the basis of his leadership of the Leningrad party apparatus. This party apparatus was formerly controlled by Malenkov, who is certainly no friend of Khrushchev. For Kozlov, hope to maintain the support of this apparatus with Khrushchev leaving the political scene seems dim.

With the correction already mentioned, the future lineup in Russia will probably see Brezhnev involved in the international aspects of Soviet policy and Kosygin the domestic aspects of Russian affairs, with Malinovsky holding the actual reins of power.

It is with the line of succession to Mao Tse-tung that I find myself in more disagreement. There is in Peking a group of Chinese marshals and generals who originally raised the flag of the Communist revolt against Chiang Kai-shek in Nanching in 1927. These soldiers—Lin Piao, Chu Teh, Chen Yi, and Chou En-lai—are a band of officers who have supplied the military thought and leadership to the Chinese Red Army since 1927, a source of power that remains under their control at the present. As the years have progressed they have risen to head the Ministry of Defense, the Red Army, the Foreign Ministry and the Premiership of the Republic. For in China, as well as in the Soviet Union, the royal road to power is through association with and control of the military, a point not well appreciated as yet by many analysts of the communist world. From the above list of officers, Chu Teh may be eliminated as a successor to Mao on the basis of his age. Chou En-lai's future success lies on his support by Lin Piao and Chen Yi, as he is the furthest of the three from the source of power, the military. In fact, my information is that the most well liked and most highly respected of this band of officers, as well as politicians, is Lin Piao. On the basis of the above reasons, my three pictures (choices) would show Lin Piao, Chen Yi, and Chou En-lai.

Sincerely,

9

SECTION II / THE RIDDLE OF SOVIET POWER: AN ANSWER TO AN ENIGMA

INTRODUCTION

The Soviet scene is an enigma because of the lack of any comprehensive theory linking the diverse events within and without Kremlin walls. During the Roman Empire there existed a Praetorian Guard whose actions not only controlled the Roman Senate but also frequently determined the election of Roman emperors. Analogously there has grown in power an elite army in Russia whose leaders have played a large role in determining the actions since 1953 of both the Presidium and the Central Committee in Moscow. This source of Soviet power allows insight into conflicts and changes within Russia.

This unbeaten group within the Soviet Armed Forces has been the Soviet Far Eastern or Siberian Army. Since 1920 leaders of this special force were Rodion Malinovsky, Ivan Konev, and Konstantin Rokossovsky. By 1957 these marshals had come to control effectively the Soviet Ministry of Defense. Through their political generals and their economic managers, they were able to extend their control over the entire spectrum of policies within the Soviet Union. Few individuals would question the military abilities of these marshals, but few individuals have been aware that these leaders were trained early in their careers as political commissars. Their teacher was Vasily K. Bleucher, who had an ability to mold men into uncommon armies and unique individuals.

Bleucher's importance is multiplied in scope, as he also created the Chinese Communist officer corps and was thus the teacher of such present-day Chinese leaders as Chou En-lai, Mao Tse-tung, Chen Yi, and Lin Piao. In short, Bleucher forged both the military doctrine and the military forces by which the Communist world survives.

An American author once complained that books written about the Soviet Union cover the country in too small sequences of scope and time. This history attempted to cover many eras of Soviet history in hopes of allowing one to grasp the simplicities and complexities of the land beyond the Iron Curtain. In this way it became possible to find a key to unlocking the riddle which is Russia.

VASILY K. BLEUCHER

The mystery which surrounds the lives of most early Communist leaders also shrouds most of the factual information concerning Vasily Bleucher. Several theories exist concerning his origin. One may say that his German name is proof that he was an ex-German officer, well versed in the mores of the German General Staff. A second may suggest that he was an ex-Tsarist officer who elected service in the new Soviet state, while a third equates his life with those of Rodion Malinovsky, Ivan Konev, and Konstantin Rokossovsky, who rose from peasant stock to become Tsarist NCOs. These three men were able to lead partisan brigades effectively although they were without formal military training. It is most likely that Bleucher was born in the Varoslav District near the Volga River in Central Russia in 1889. He worked in a locomotive factory and, for his part in a factory strike in 1910, was sentenced to over two years' imprisonment. His revolutionary tendencies increased during his jail term, for prison became to Bleucher, as it has for many other leaders of the twentieth century, an institution of great education. After his release Bleucher was drafted and served in the Tsarist army where he was wounded and later cited for bravery. In St. Petersburg he helped organize the Petrograd Soviet whose members, along with their Siberian battalion supporters, were instrumental in overthrowing both the tsar and the Provisional Government of Alexander Kerensky.

Bleucher later joined the Samara Revolutionary Committee, commanding military detachments in victories against Dutov, a White Russian leader. In 1918 Bleucher was the first Russian to receive the Order of the Red Banner for his military prowess. During the European Russian Civil War, he commanded the "Iron Division" against the offensive of Admiral Aleksandr Kolchak and General Petr Wrangel. These successful commands early in the Civil War led to Trotsky's appointment of this young leader as commander of the partisan bands in Siberia. From 1921 to 1923 Bleucher saved the Far East for the Soviets. His newly trained revolutionary armies defeated Cossack Atamen Semenov, forced the evacuation of the Japanese, and ended Allied intervention in Siberia. It is not hard to imagine that his viewing of the Siberian troops both in Petrograd and in the Far East led him to believe that it was these men through whom he could build an elite army to defend the new Soviet state both in peace and in war.

Bleucher's greatest victory in European Russia was the defeat of the forces of General Wrangel in the Crimea. Across the Isthmus of Crimea, only four miles wide at high tide, Bleucher's Iron Division smashed through to conquer the Crimea. This tactic was successfully copied in 1941 by the acknowledged leading German commander of troops, General Erich Von Mannstein. During this period in European Russia (1918–20), Bleucher was masked to increase his mystery, and it was at this time that he took the name Bleucher from Napoleon's archenemy, General Blücher of Prussia.

At the end of the Siberian episode in 1922, Bleucher returned to Moscow to assist Trotsky in the reorganization of the Red Army. In Moscow, Bleucher was instrumental in starting the Red Military Academy, later called the Frunze Military Academy. Here Bleucher, under Lenin and Trotsky's approval, expounded the doctrines of Clausewitz. Other teachers, such as Boris M. Shaposhnikov, carried this tradition forward to World War II.

Many of the top-ranking military leaders of the Soviet Union graduated from the Frunze Military Academy. These Frunze students included Zhukov in 1924, Konev in 1926, Rokossovsky in 1929, and Malinovsky in 1930. At Frunze, a new unified proletarian military doctrine was taught, which was Clausewitz modified by Marx, Lenin, and Bleucher. During this stay in Moscow in 1922, ties were begun with the German military establishment, allowing both countries to test weaponry within the Russian borders and to cross-fertilize each other with ideas concerning the new armored warfare.

Bleucher's talents for political organization should not go unrecognized. In 1921 he sent to Outer Mongolia a mission under Rokossovsky, firmly establishing the military and political ties of the new nation to the Soviet Union. The Soviet indoctrination of the native leaders of Outer Mongolia left the nation politically and militarily tied to Russia and beyond the Chinese sphere of influence. Between 1938 and 1945, these ties were reinforced during the Russo-Japanese conflicts. By 1961, Soviet support had led to the admission of Outer Mongolia to the United Nations.

Bleucher appeared only briefly on the stage of Chinese politics, but his influence in modern Chinese history was as great in scope as it was in Russia. It was because of Lenin's and Trotsky's interest in disseminating the Russian Revolution to other countries that Bleucher was sent to China. In 1922, the Chinese revolutionary government of Dr. Sun Yat-sen was struggling to survive in the face of opposition by warlords who either rose to power as a result of the support they received from Japanese or German economic interests in China or who had maintained their power after the fall of the Manchu dynasty. It was these powerful warlords, protecting their economic interests, who had driven Dr. Sun's Kuomintang party to Canton in Southern China. Some supporters of the Chinese Revolution, already indoctrinated in the teachings of Marx, turned to the Russians to save Dr. Sun's government. The appeal was answered first by sending a Soviet mission under the leadership of Adolph Joffe, an ally of Lenin and Trotsky, to the Kuomintang.

Joffe, speaking to Dr. Sun, promised Russian military and

13

economic aid to ensure the success of the Chinese Revolution. This revolution was to be sponsored under Dr. Sun's three principles, which were not unlike the Bolshevik principles of peace, land, and bread. Because the Soviet economy had been crippled by the Russian Civil War, the Russians sent men and ideas rather than money to foster revolution. These men were Bleucher, Mikhail Borodin, Adolph Joffe, and Vasily Chuikov. To Bleucher now fell the task of creating a successful Kuomintang army. Chiang Kai-shek had been sent by Dr. Sun to view Soviet progress and learn the lessons of revolution. He was so impressed with Bluecher's military knowledge that he specifically requested Bluecher to come to China to train Dr. Sun's troops.

Bleucher, establishing a model army, first created an officer corps, steeped in revolutionary doctrine. To this end, the Whampoa Military Academy was established in Canton, an academy at which many of the future Nationalist and Communist Chinese officers were to learn the fundamentals of a people's war. A roster of the Whampoa Academy included among others Chiang Kai-shek as commandant, Chou En-lai as secretary of the academy, and Lin Piao as cadet and honor officer. Assigned to the propaganda section of the academy was a militant union organizer named Mao Tse-tung. Political lectures at the academy were provided by Mikhail Borodin.

Although Dr. Sun's death soon followed the arrival of the Soviet advisors, it was they who supplied the cohesiveness that allowed an orderly succession to Chiang Kai-shek. Sun Yat-sen's traditions in the Communist movement in China were maintained by Madame Sun Yat-sen, today a vice-premier in Communist China and a sister-in-law of Chiang Kai-shek.

In Canton, Bleucher was known by his pseudonym Galen, after the Roman medical teacher. By 1925 the Whampoa cadets were attacked by a counterrevolutionary force led by an ex-Kuomintang general and warlord. Through this attack, Galen remained by a telephone, acting as both intelligence coordinator and commander of the new army. He directed the cadets and other revolutionary soldiers through the Canton streets to victory. From the time he received news of the warlord's advance and throughout that night and the following day, Bleucher led, cajoled, and directed, emerging victorious. With his victory, Bleucher knew that the time for training had ended; the time to march had come. After two years of preparation, the campaign to the north began in 1926.

Bleucher had trained more than 10,000 future military and political leaders. He and Borodin planned to send some of these men, disguised as peasants, to announce the nature of the revolution to the people. The people were promised peace, land, and bread; in return, many joined the movement as guerrillas. The Northern Expedition was thus able to gather momentum and sweep the stronger armies of the warlords before them. During the advance, the political and military agents of the Kuomintang did their propaganda work well ahead of the army. Undefeated, the Kuomintang armies were able to rest before Shanghai. Because of the advance work of Chou En-lai, the city was already in Kuomintang hands before the army even entered it.

During 1926, the year of the Northern Expedition, Galen presumably fell ill and returned to the Soviet Union for medical care. In his absence, internecine strife broke out in the ranks of the Kuomintang. The organization developed into pro-Communist and moderate factions. Chiang had attempted first to mollify the extremists of both the moderate and left wings of the Kuomintang. By 1926 Chiang foresaw more danger coming from the pro-Communist faction, and, in Galen's absence, he executed some of the extremists. Before further strife ensued, Galen returned with more Soviet military aid which almost served to pacify the situation. However, the damage was done, and the left Kuomintang established a provisional government in Hankow along the Yangtse River. The leftist government started to develop a separate army in order not to depend on Chiang and to conquer Northern China independently. Outside Shanghai, in Nanchang, Chiang listened in secret to the messengers of the concessionaires of Shanghai. The foreign bankers, fearing the Communists more than they feared Chiang Kai-shek, supposedly offered him $50,000,000 for his treasury and $7,000,000 a month to pay his troops if he would destroy the Communist element in the Kuomintang. Facing a leftist government in Hangkow and a Communist element in Shanghai, Chiang acted to protect his position. After he had sent Galen away from his Whampoa-led troops, Chiang felt free to turn on the Communists. He either slaughtered or exiled many of them in Shanghai, and later, with the help of the Manchurian warlord Chang Tso-lin, he destroyed the power of the left Kuomintang in Hankow. Although Bleucher's position was precarious, Chiang allowed him to be recalled to the Soviet Union without incident.

Galen had spent two years teaching the Chinese revolutionaries, and he remained respected by both sides. Lin Piao later stated that he had learned all his lessons from General Galen; Chiang Kai-shek requested Bleucher's return to China many times between 1927 and 1937, until Vasily Chuikov was sent in Bleucher's place. Chiang always believed that Bleucher was disinterested in the factionalism within the Kuomintang during 1926 and 1927. Chiang felt the Chinese Communists had tried to destroy his rule due to the individual greed of the left Kuomintang leaders. Perhaps Chiang felt that if Bleucher had not become ill in 1926, an accommodation would have been worked out which would have led to a democratic China. By 1927 there was no role left for Bleucher to play other than an apolitical one.

Although Chiang attempted to destroy the political influence of both the Russian and Chinese Communist leaders, he was helped by no less a figure than Stalin. Far from the Chinese scene in Moscow, Stalin was embroiled in controversy with Trotsky. Stalin supported Chiang, still believing that Chiang was loyal to him and distrustful of Trotsky and his allies. Thus, Stalin tied the hands of the Russian advisors at Hankow in their plans to destroy Chiang and left the field open for Chiang to destroy the left Kuomintang. Among the leaders of the left Kuomintang who were thus forced into temporary obscurity were Madame Sun Yat-sen and her brother, T. V. Soong. Even Borodin in Hankow was reduced to inactivity, confusion, and despair.

The failure of the Hankow government and the loss of contact with Moscow left Bleucher's various Chinese Whampoa students free to act. They were the personally trained cadets by whom Bleucher's teachings were actually carried. Many joined Chiang's ranks, while others, individually at first and then in increasing numbers, attempted to raise and spread a true Communist revolution. In Central and Southern China occurred the sporadic revolts which led, after many years, to the final Communist triumph in China.

In Central China two Whampoa luminaries were in revolt. Secretary of the Academy Chou En-lai had gone to Shanghai to organize an insurrection in the city before the arrival of Chiang's forces. Outside the city with Chiang's troops was Colonel Lin Piao. After Shanghai fell and the counterrevolution had begun, Chou and Lin fled with their troops to Nanchang where other pupils of Galen controlled the garrison. At Nanchang, Chen-Yi, an exemplary student from Whampoa, had established a military academy similar to Whampoa. In this way Galen had hoped to continue to train a nucleus of officers needed for the further campaign in China. Another leader of both the Nanchang garrison and the school was Chu Teh who, under the guidance of Chen-Yi and others, had become a staunch Communist. Parts of the garrison and the military academy rose at Nanchang. This revolt has come to be considered the first true Communist insurrection in China. The leaders of this revolt were Chou En-lai, Lin Piao, Chu Teh, and Chen Yi, now united in the Communist cause. Chiang acted quickly from Shanghai, dispatching troops which were able to contain the rebellion and force the flight of the four revolution leaders and their armies to South China. In the south was Mao Tse-tung who, with some Whampoa cadets, had fled Canton to the rural belt of China. While Chiang busied himself putting down the Nanchang rebellion and other rebellions in the center of China, Mao was able to establish the first Chinese Soviet. It was to this Chinese Soviet that the four Nanchang leaders fled. Between 1927 and 1931 these leaders organized large areas and a nascent peasant army under the Communist banner. The spokesman for the revolution was Chou En-lai; the writer and philosopher of the revolution was Mao Tse-tung. The army commander was Chu Teh, assisted by Chen Yi, and the recognized military tactician was Lin Piao.

Lin Piao was the son of a factory owner ruined by the taxation of the various warlords. After his appointment to Whampoa as a cadet, he came under the influence of Galen. By 1927 and the march northward, Lin Piao was a colonel at age twenty. He fought well from Canton to Hankow and then to Shanghai on the Yangtze. Following the Nanchang uprising, Lin established officer schools wherever the Chinese Communist Army was to be. In 1937 he was the principal of the Yennan Military Academy, which trained officers for the growing Red armies in China, and was reputed never to have lost a battle in more than 100 military actions. By 1931, in the disagreements between Moscow and the so-called agrarian Chinese, Mao and his followers were trying to disengage themselves from any Russian influence. Many times Stalin attempted to place new leaders within the Communist movements in Chinese cities, but each attempt would fail in the cities while Mao's rural-based revolution continued to prosper. The conflict between Mao and Moscow led Mao to adapt the trappings of a Confucian scholar and the military philosophy of Sun Tze, a Chinese sage of 500 B.C., thereby adding emotional heritage to the Chinese Revolution, replacing a living Russian military tactician with a Chinese philosopher of war, and eliminating all vestiges of Russian influence in the Chinese Revolution. It was not until after World War II that Stalin and Mao reached an understanding to act in concert as brothers, but this unity has not withstood the test of time.

BLEUCHER IN SIBERIA

The creation of the Siberian Army was, for Bleucher, both a deterrent against foreign aggression in the Far East, whether Chinese or Japanese, and a military-political melting pot for the Siberian peoples, whether Mongol, Manchu, or Tartar.

The autonomous status of the Siberian Army recognized that this army would have to fight alone for long periods without reinforcement from European Russia. The first Russo-Japanese War in 1905 had shown the inadequacy of the Trans-

Siberian Railroad in supplying the Far Eastern front during large-scale war. To prevent Siberian dependency on a questionable railroad system during wartime, the Siberian Army was allowed to build local munitions, airplane, and tank factories, as well as set up supply depots and air bases. From 1923 on, industrialization continued apace under the direction of Aleksei Kosygin.

In 1929 Bleucher's army was challenged by the Manchurian warlord Chang Hsueh-liang, popularly known as Young Marshal Chang. After the assassination of his father Chang Tso-lin, Young Marshal Chang ousted the Soviets from their Northern Manchurian Railroad concessions. At first the Soviet Union averred disinterest in the railway in an attempt to placate the Chinese. The Siberian Army was alerted, but no retaliatory action was taken. Young Marshal Chang, encouraged by the successful takeover of the railroad, next attempted to annex disputed Manchurian-Siberian border areas. At the border his Manchurian troops were driven back and Chang's empire began to crumble. Chang Hsueh-liang's troops, now demoralized, lost to the Japanese only two years later. For its battle action in 1929 the Siberian Army was given the title of Far Eastern Red Banner Army. From 1930 to 1935 Bleucher's army was involved in border wars throughout the long Sino-Soviet Frontier. Other marauding warlords in Siberia received no welcome from the Red Banner Army.

The title "Banner Army" is interesting in that it comes from the Manchu term for an elite fighting force. The Manchus, conquerors of China, referred to their best troops as Banner Armies, and it was these troops which garrisoned the more important Chinese cities and supported the native puppet leadership. Originally no ranks were accorded to military leaders in the Soviet Union, but, as the Soviet armies grew in strength, recognition of individual accomplishments dictated the necessity of officer ranks. In fact, Bleucher was one of the first five Soviet officers to achieve marshal's rank (1935) and one of the few to achieve that early rank for military achievement.

Other officers who rapidly rose in rank in the Siberian Army were Malinovsky, Rokossovsky and Konev. Rokossovsky, of

Polish origin, distinguished himself as a NCO in the Tsarist army. He joined the Red Guard in 1919 and distinguished himself in action against Admiral Kolchak. Under Bleucher's leadership in the Far East, he fought Atamen Semenov and entered Mongolia in pursuit of Baron Ungern-Sternberg, another White Russian general. Rokossovsky gained further distinction in action against Young Marshal Chang and rose to corps commander in 1937.

Ivan Konev, the son of an impoverished peasant, was drafted into the Tsarist army and became an early Communist party organizer. In the Civil War, Konev fought against the Whites in European Russian provinces as commissar of Armored Train 102. This armored train was similar to Trotsky's own armored train. By 1922 Konev was a division commander under Bleucher, taking part in battles against Semenov and the Japanese. By the 1930s he was second in command to Bleucher in the Far East. By 1938, Malinovsky (a general in Siberia), Rokossovsky, and Konev had each served more than fifteen years in military apprenticeship to Bleucher. Siberia had not been an exile. Stalin, apparently jealous of the power of the new Soviet officer class, began the famous army purges in 1936. From 1936 to 1938 Stalin destroyed a majority of his officers.

Perhaps Bleucher, Rokossovsky, Malinovsky, and Konev were able to survive the purge of 1936 because they were in Spain. Stalin's help to Loyalist Spain came in the form of the International Brigade and tank commanders. When Franco's forces advanced to the outskirts of Madrid, a determined contingent of the International Brigade led by General Klèber stopped their advance. Just as Bleucher had taken the name of the Prussian military commander foremost against Napoleon, in Madrid he took the name Klèber, the man whom he considered Napoleon's best general prior to 1800. As Klèber he stated that he was really a Hungarian named Lazar Stern and he spoke in German. If Rokossovsky, Konev, and Malinovsky were in Spain as tank advisors, it could have been none other than Bleucher. In Spain Bleucher had chosen the name of a republican French general of the revolution, and, as Klèber, he suggested military academies and other reforms to the loyalist government.

For his efforts, Klèber was rebuffed and removed from the International Brigade and inadvertently allowed to lead one of the few victories of the Loyalist cause along the Ebo River. In 1938, as Stern, he was allowed to return to Siberia.

After his return to Siberia in 1938, Stern or Bleucher disappeared during the Stalinist purges. Chiang Kai-shek learned, but disbelieved, that Galen had been executed for consorting with a Japanese woman spy. However, Stalin had finally struck out against the strength and popularity of Marshal Bleucher. To destroy Bleucher the services of Marshal Voroshilov were necessary. As Stalin's hatchet man, Voroshilov visited Siberia with Georgi Zhukov in 1938. Bleucher died; Rokossovsky, Malinovsky, and Konev lived. Their survival was due, in part perhaps, to the Japanese buildup in the Far East. The Japanese war against China was bound to lead to conflict with the Soviets. However, there is some question as to the acquiescence of the Siberian people and officer corps toward Bleucher's death.

Perhaps the tremendous economic gains made in the areas of agriculture, transportation, and industry by the Siberian peoples since the Civil War helped them maintain their allegiance to Stalin, the former minister for national minorities, or perhaps the report of Bleucher's death was only a ruse.

Marshal Voroshilov had stirred many feelings by removing Bleucher, for Bleucher was a legendary teacher and military organizer. His apt pupils, Konev, Rokossovsky, and Malinovsky, kept dissatisfaction quiet for many years before the 1960s, when they effectively downgraded Voroshilov for his role in Siberia. In 1938, the hand of Stalin was just too powerful and General Zhukov did not make enemies among his new Siberian Army subordinates. Rokossovsky did incur Stalin's displeasure and was later relieved of his corps command and placed in jail. For Rokossovsky, an outspoken man, temporary torture, imprisonment, and retirement from the army were the orders of the day. Even under torture by the Secret Police, he refused to betray other army officers during the purge. This feature of his life supposedly led to the high respect which members of the Soviet Army held for him.

Georgi Zhukov, the new commander, had been conscripted during World War I into the Tsarist army, where he was known as a brave and outstanding soldier. He deserted the Tsarist army for the Revolution, joining the early Red Army Cavalry in 1917 and the Communist party in 1919. Zhukov came to Stalin's attention during the Civil War in the fighting around Tsaritsyn, later called Stalingrad. For his successful adventures during the Civil War, Zhukov was given successive posts of military importance. For further military and political indoctrination, he attended the Frunze Military Academy under Shaposhnikov, who did not consider Zhukov among his brightest pupils. When World War II came, it was Shaposhnikov who recommended the recall of Konev, Malinovsky, and Rokossovsky from retirement to lead the troops before Moscow. Because of their successes under trying conditions in the front at Moscow, Zhukov could not replace these generals. Soon after, however, as commander of the Russian armies, Zhukov announced the retirement of Shaposhnikov for reasons of ill health.

Part of Zhukov's responsibility in Siberia was to prevent further dissatisfaction within the Siberian Army. He appeared to be gentle because he did not purge officers other than Bleucher, Rokossovsky, and certain air force officers. The well-trained Bleucher officer corps remained intact, although in temporary eclipse, in Siberia. Stalin's actions in Siberia were in contrast to the 1936–38 decimation of the Soviet officer corps of the other army groups. This policy might have resulted from the need for an effective army in Siberia dictated by Japanese provocations. Further, in 1938 the Siberian Army contained one third of the Soviet armed forces and thus, without the Siberian Army officer corps, there would have been no experienced field commanders left after the purges.

Marshal Bleucher's legacy was the most stable and best trained of the Soviet armies. This statement can best be appreciated in a discussion of the Second Russo-Japanese War in 1938 and 1939 and the days preceding World War II. But first, a digression will show that it was Bleucher's teachings which guided the Siberian and Chinese Communist armies in battle.

BLEUCHER'S THEORETICAL LEGACY

Bleucher's military tactics, successfully developed and used in China and Siberia, were, in effect, a Communist translation of the Clausewitzian doctrines from *On War*. Bleucher's genius lay in bringing these military theories to the new Red armies. Perhaps Bleucher's introduction to *On War* came from the interest of Karl Marx, Lenin, and Trotsky in the work. In *On War*, a German military strategist spoke of a people's war in which an armed national population was in battle against a foreign aggressor force. Clausewitz had viewed the tactics of General Mikhail I. Kutuzov in the fields and snow-covered plains of Russia as well as those of the Spanish partisan bands coordinated by the Duke of Wellington. These campaigns, which led to the defeat of Napoleon, were seen as lessons of future military significance. Clausewitz felt that the era of limited war had ended with the rise and fall of Napoleon. Lenin accepted Clausewitz's doctrines by considering a class war a people's war, and Lenin and Trotsky both accepted Clausewitz's concept that an offensive war was a weaker form of combat than a defensive war. Clausewitz had seen that victory could no longer be based on the offensive which could be ended by a single battle, but rather on an elastic defense based on retreating into the interior, maintaining a concentration of forces, creating a people's war to provide the necessary reserve manpower, initiating multiple counterattacks, maintaining the mobility of pursuit, and maintaining the element of surprise.

Clausewitz also held that war in the military and the political spheres was an organic whole from which single members could not be separated. In the Soviet Union, war, then, became the continuation of politics by violent means. Military leaders and Communist party members were partners in the master strategy of the state. The action of each soldier was a political as well as a military movement. To foster this tenet of war, the Soviets developed the political commissar for the military system. Bleucher considered the best military leader to be the general who was as adept politically as he was militarily.

As the action of each soldier became political as well as military, both Russia and China advanced the role of the lowly infantry soldier to that of queen of the army. As each new tactical weapon was introduced, it became subordinate to, and supportive of, the infantry soldier. The tank, the airplane, artillery, the rocket, etc., were under the overall command of the infantry general who best understood the average soldier.

Contrast this practice with that of the divided American Joint Chiefs of Staff, where each major service branch attempts to place its own particular ideas first. In light of the Clausewitzian doctrine, controversies such as the role of the aircraft carrier versus the land-based bomber in war were easily settled. It would be the Soviet infantry general who would evaluate each new weapon in terms of its value to the infantry.

Lin Piao, in the Communist encampments around Yennan in the middle 1930s, stressed these principles of war. (These principles will at times be commented upon for their relevance.)

1. *The partisan army is to refuse any engagement until there are strong indications of success in battle, for the partisans cannot afford to lose.*

2. *Surprise is the main offensive tactic of the partisans and position warfare or static warfare is to be avoided.*

Comment: The avoidance of static warfare came from a belief in the superiority of a mobile or elastic defensive military posture. General Heinz Guderian, a friend of Bleucher, stressed the importance of surprise and mobility. Guderian served as the military instructor of the renascent German army after World War I as well as instructor of a number of Soviet officers in 1922 in the Russian testing grounds where post-World War I German equipment was tested beyond the sight of the Allies. Guderian later successfully practiced surprise and mobility in Russia and learned that defense was more powerful than offense in the snows of Russia in 1941.

3. *Any attack or retreat must be detailed and open to the knowledge of all the partisans.*

Comment: Here Clausewitz concentrated on the importance of the individual soldier in fighting the battle. By making each soldier cognizant of his role in battle, the Red theorists hoped to maintain the highest morale among the men. During the later stages of the Korean conflict, spies would report to the American command full details of impending Chinese Communist attacks. The spies had gained this information simply by sitting in at military and political group discussions with Chinese infantry soldiers.

4. *Every peasant is a friend, every landlord an enemy.*

Comment: Lenin figures prominently here by making the people's war a class war. In addition, this dictum called for the military destruction of the enemy's base of support, which was so necessary for victory. Lin Piao stressed to his men the importance in their dealings with the peasants of paying for food, treating women with respect, and rolling up their bedrolls after having used the peasant's hut. Along with these instructions to the soldiers were messages of political indoctrination for the peasant. The peasant then often became influential in deciding the tide of battle.

5. *The partisans are to avoid battle if the enemy has greater manpower. However, the goal of a highly experienced partisan force is "short attacks" against thousands of the enemy in a vulnerable position.*

Comment: Surprise and concentration of forces are stressed here. Other military leaders such as Brigadier Orville Wingate in Burma against the Japanese, or Gideon in Israel against the Medianites, had successfully utilized these principles in war. The "short attack" was preached by Lin Piao and applied by Chu Teh's partisans. Marine General Frank Carlson, who had been in China, used this principle with his first Marine Raider Battalion against the Japanese.

6. *The partisans' defensive line should be open to the greatest elasticity.*

Comment: This clearly stresses defense in depth and maneuverability.

7. *Partisan tactics consist of decoy, feint, ambush, distraction, and irritation.*

Comment: For the Chinese, these tactics were "the principle of pretending to attack the east while attacking the west."

8. *The partisans are to engage only the weakest links of the most vital parts of the enemy's army.*

9. *Mobility coordinated with well worked out plans for dispersal are as important as the actual plans for meeting an enemy advance.*

Comment: Mobility of an army was of special importance to Communist leaders. Infantrymen should be able to walk more than forty miles a day. The partisans could thus take advantage of more ambitious maneuvering plans than could their enemies, who were able to move only twenty miles daily. Full plans for pursuit or retreat, along with superior mobility, allowed the Communist generals a full concentration of forces at all times.

10. *The partisans must gain the full confidence of the people and the people must be won over politically. The people then become the intelligence network of the army.*

Comment: The core of a people's war is the connection of the armed struggle with the goals of the people. Those commanders who can impart these precepts of war build for themselves the support of the peasant masses. Paraphrased by Mao Tse-tung, this concept is like being the "fish in the sea." As the Communist army expands its control over an area, political training to develop new leaders accompanies every phase of the struggle to further the revolutionary cause.

Bleucher's teachings demonstrated that it was no shame for soldiers to retreat, to harass, to outmaneuver, and to lose land to the enemy. Even cities were unimportant for, like jails, they imprisoned people. The Siberian and Chinese Communists took six and twenty years, respectively, to win against overwhelming odds. In a period of ten years, Bleucher had created two of the most powerful armies of the twentieth century, the Red Banner Siberian Army and the Chinese Eighth Route Army. The victory of the Chinese Eighth Route Army against the Kuomintang from Manchuria to Hainan Island is a story separate from that of the Siberian Army and perhaps more readily appreciated and known. The next chapters will describe the Siberian Army as a fighting force and then as the dominant political reality in the Soviet Union in the 1960s.

PRELUDE TO WAR

The years preceding World War II appear, in retrospect, to be a pattern of offensive and defensive moves testing out potential enemies. The first to test the Soviet mettle was the Japanese army in the Second Russo-Japanese War. Imperialistically minded Japan had destroyed Russian influence in Korea and Southern Manchuria in 1905. Subsequently, with the Russian and the Chinese revolutions in the 1920s, the Soviets had lost influence over Northern Manchuria. The "Rising Sun" filled the power void and, by 1931, completed the economic domination of all Manchuria by creating the political fiction of Manchukuo. The extension of the Japanese borders by the addition of Manchukuo placed Japanese soldiers facing the Maritime Provinces as well as the Russian-organized state of Outer Mongolia. Bleucher's army, the Far Eastern Red Banner Army, under Georgi Zhukov, faced the Kwantung Army, considered the finest of Japanese armies, far from the eyes of Western observers.

The Kwantung Army had been the conqueror of Manchuria. Generals Doihara, Itagak, and Ishihara, who led the secret police, the army, and the army operations department, respectively, were the men most responsible for Japan's Asiatic military movements. The word "Kwantung" (border province) refers to the Kwantung Peninsula leading to Darien and Port Arthur.

Watching the turmoil created by the Chinese Revolution, the Japanese aggressively coveted certain Chinese territories. During the Chinese Revolution, when Marshal Chang Tso-lin raised the Kuomintang banner over Mukden in 1927, the Japanese generals viewed a united China as a threat to their future plans. To counter the Kuomintang expansion. General Doihara had Marshal Chang Tso-lin assassinated on the Japanese-controlled part of the Manchurian Railroad. However, Young Marshal Chang, the son of Chang Tso-lin, took over his father's army, foiling the first Japanese plot. In 1931, on the pretext that the Young Marshal's soldiers had killed Japanese soldiers, the Kwantung Army marched into Manchuria, completing their initial imperialistic aims.

27

The Kwantung Army remained on the offensive and, by 1937, had marched into the Chinese Northeastern Provinces and Shanghai. This army provoked many incidents along the Siberian border between 1936 and 1939. One such incident was Japan's claim to the region overlooking the heights of Lake Kassam, south of Vladivostok. In 1938 a Japanese division was dispatched across the Eastern Manchurian border to annex this portion of Siberian territory. This division of the Kwantung Army seized the heights quickly in a "sneak attack." In retaliation, a Siberian Army division was dispatched within three days. Supported by artillery, tanks, and planes, this division was able to drive the Japanese back into Manchuria after a short battle. The Soviet use of planes, tanks, and artillery in a small border war points to the high degree of military sophistication within the Far Eastern Army (Siberian Army).

In 1939, following the Soviet officer purges, the Japanese decided to retest the Soviet armed strength. The Japanese attempted to overthrow Russian influence in Outer Mongolia by moving an enlarged (for that time) army group of 250,000 men of the Kwantung Army to a disputed border area between May and September, 1939. The actual battle occurred at Khalkin Gol along the Mongol-Manchurian border. Preliminaries included air battles as well as cavalry skirmishes. The Japanese base of attack was only forty miles from the major Japanese railroad depot. The Siberian Army under Zhukov consisted of a similar-sized army group whose supply base was 500 miles from the front lines. The Siberian Army was augmented by the cavalry and the infantry of the Outer Mongolian Republic. Integration of these units created no problems as the Mongolian officers had been trained by Bleucher and his generals.

Zhukov's army utilized speed and mechanized power to defend against the Japanese provocations in Outer Mongolia. In the battle which followed, Zhukov's forces effectively utilized tanks and cavalry in a pre-World War II blitzkrieg attack to outflank and outfight the advancing Japanese. The Kwantung Army was crushed, and few survivors of this offensive action reached Manchukuo. The Japanese sued for a truce which led, in 1941, to a nonaggression pact with the Soviets. Due to Zhukov's victory over the Japanese in Outer Mongolia, the eastern marches of the Soviet Union were secured for the duration of World War II. Instead, the Japanese moved to Southeast Asia to satisfy their need for a place in the sun.

In the West the Siberian Army made its first appearance in Finland. Strategic considerations showed that, before World War II, Hitler had attempted to mollify the threat of Soviet power by concluding a Russo-German nonaggression pact. The Germans conceded to the Soviets considerable territory along the Baltic coast and in Poland, although the Germans themselves were not yet in control of the land.

After the 1939 war with Poland, the Soviets became acutely aware of the threat of a German invasion which could be launched along the common Russo-German frontier. Uppermost in Soviet minds was the weak defensive position of the city of Leningrad. The Soviets knew that the northern approaches to the city were open to attack by land from Finland and Estonia and by sea from the Gulf of Finland.

The Russian leadership, professing to neutralize the attempt by an invader to utilize the invasion routes to Leningrad, forced a pact for mutual defense upon the border states of Latvia, Estonia, Lithuania, and Finland. Latvia, Estonia, and Lithuania capitulated to the Soviet gestures and, within a year, they were strategically occupied by Soviet troops. The Soviets offered Finland a mutual defense pact which would have allowed the Soviets to garrison various land and naval bases within Finland, to protect the sea and land approaches to Leningrad. When the mutual defense pact was rejected by Finnish leadership, the Finnish military began a full mobilization, bringing 500,000 men and women into the Finnish army. The Soviet Union launched five armies totalling 600,000 men against the Finnish border. The Finnish front consisted of both the Mannerheim Line, a defensive position in depth north of Leningrad, and the much larger eastern Russo-Finnish frontier.

Finnish partisans reported massive onslaughts of Soviet troops combined with air raids, massed artillery, and an unsuccessful

Communist revolution within Finland. The Finns claimed great victories and correspondingly great Soviet losses. In the winter, Finnish bobsleds, manned by courageous machinegunners, played havoc with the Russian forces. The Finns rose to the occasion, driving the Russians back to their trenches to the tune of "Finlandia." Heroic individual Finnish marksmen pinned down whole divisions of Soviet troops. In the end, however, the crushing number of Soviet troops destroyed the Finnish resistance.

Perhaps the tactical consideration and evidence are slightly different from the above description. The Russo-Finnish War consisted of three phases, the first in December, 1939; the second in January, 1940; and the third in February and March, 1940. An offensive war is usually won by a better than three-to-one advantage in men and firepower. Because the number of combatants utilized in the first phase of the war was equal, the Russian invasion cannot be called a major offensive action. The Soviets originally fought for minor territorial gains, hoping for a rapid peace.

When a treaty of peace was not signed, the Soviets sent larger units from other military districts to the front line. In January, Ukrainians first appeared as soldiers on the front line. The second phase of the war brought large Russian losses, because the Soviet forces were untrained for winter warfare.

The third phase of the war, taking place during February and March, happened at a time when the war was a worldwide concern. Over 10,000 foreign volunteers and up to 1,000 trained fighter pilots were to—or had—joined Finland's defense. For the Soviets, a decisive victory in January took on increasing importance, before Britain, France, or even Germany united with the Finns against the Soviets. To accomplish a quick victory, Marshal Timoshenko, Soviet chief for the Finnish operations, was replaced by General Zhukov, and Timoshenko's troops were replaced by the Siberian Army units, already well accustomed to fighting in winter climates. Timoshenko's failure was during the second phase (the January phase) of the war. In February and March the fresh Siberian units arrived and were committed to the assault upon the Mannerheim Line. In March the Mannerheim Line was turned and Finnish resistance collapsed under the tactics of the Siberian Army.

The tactical use of Siberian troops under General Zhukov was the clue to unraveling the nature of the Soviet victory in Finland. To Bleucher's soldiers, a frontal assault could only occur when the enemy was mortally weakened or victory was inevitable. To bring about a weakening of Finnish morale, Siberian troops were trained in individual and patrol infiltration. The Siberians, trained in camouflage, discarded the Russian military gray uniforms for snow-white winter uniforms. The outflanking operations on the Finnish positions met with success and brought about the close of the war in Finland. If the Finnish solder had proved his excellence in the Russo-Finnish War, then the Siberian soldier was even better. The Siberian Army, which had proved itself against the Japanese and Finns, was next to prove itself against the Germans in World War II. Zhukov, for his victory in Finland, was brought to Moscow to organize the Soviet defensive posture. The actual victors in Finland, the Siberian Army, returned to the Maritime Provinces to counter any further Japanese ambitions towards the Soviet Union.

WORLD WAR II AND THE SIBERIAN ARMY

A study of the Soviet-German conflict between June 22, 1941, and May 8, 1945, begins with the tactical implications of the war and leads to the more individualized implications of these tactics on the battlefield. One principle which stands out is that an offensive action, to achieve a victory, needs at least three soldiers on the offensive to one on the defensive. This principle holds also for the ratio between offensive and defensive firepower. A mobilized army group for either the Russians or the Germans in World War II was approximately 600,000 men. Each army group consisted of four to six armies of 100,000 or more men each. (The Soviet Army Group and the German Army Group will be abbreviated SAG and GAG, respectively, with the name of the leader or the location of the army group following the abbreviation.)

In 1941 Hitler considered Russia the only European power capable of contesting his ambitions for European domination. England was isolated while Europe was under Nazi rule. Operation Barbarossa, the attack on the Soviet Union, was launched by Hitler to destroy the Soviet power. It followed the German pacification of the Balkans earlier in 1941. The German strategy of invasion was based on three objectives: Leningrad in northern Russia, Moscow in central European Russia, and the Ukraine and the oilfields of the Donets Basin in southern Russia. The Germans prepared three army groups: GAG North pointed at Leningrad, GAG Center pointed at Moscow, and GAG South pointed at the Ukraine.

GAG North contained three German armies, including one panzer or tank army, in Prussia and three mixed Finnish and German armies in Finland. GAG Center contained three infantry armies and two mobile panzer armies to bolster the armed might of the center. GAG South also contained one panzer army and five infantry armies bolstered in the Balkans by reserves of more than 260,000 men. The three GAGs plus the immediate reserve of the GAG South totalled 2,000,000 men. Other ample reserves, garrisoned in the Balkans and supplied by vassal states, replaced the German manpower expended in the original offensive and were utilized to form a second GAG South for an offensive against Stalingrad in 1942.

The Soviets faced westward with three army groups. In June, 1941, these three SAGs were not fully mobilized and existed at one third of their full mobilized strength. Other SAGs guarded the Persian, Turkish, Chinese, and Manchurian borders, and these reserves were to be initially committed piecemeal as replacements. At the Soviet border, then, were three peacetime groups totalling 600,000 men. The German superiority in 1941 was greater than the three-to-one ratio needed for successful offensive action.

From June through the summer months, the Germans were able to utilize their manpower advantage. The advance of GAG Center was impeded when the highly mobile panzer armies were diverted to reinforce the offensives of GAG North and GAG South late in the summer of 1941. These panzer armies maintained German offensive superiority on the flanks, inflicting heavy losses on the opposing but growing Russian army. Soviet manpower proved expendable, and more than 1,000,000 Soviet soldiers were sent out of action in the summer months of 1941; one million others were to be lost during the autumn of 1941. By November, 1941, the Soviets replaced the losses of the three SAGs and brought them to full strength. By November, 1941, GAG North, GAG Center, and GAG South totalled 1,800,000 men. In that month the Soviets boasted as many frontline men as the Germans. This equalization of Soviet-German forces effectively neutralized the German offensive, but during November, 1941, the Soviets brought to the central or Moscow front two additional army groups from the large Soviet reserve in the east. The Soviet General Staff did not commit these men, numbering over a million, immediately to the battlefield but held them in reserve until the German advance was within forty miles of Moscow.

On December 6–7, 1941, the Soviets opened the second phase of the war with an offensive along the central front. They enjoyed a three-to-one superiority over the Germans and swept the Germans back until the winter of 1942 forced an end to the activities of this phase of the war.

In May, 1942, the Germans gathered armies of Italians, Rumanians, Spaniards, and Germans to form a second GAG South. This German offensive had Stalingrad as its goal. The Russian Army Group facing the German offensive had not been reinforced and faced the west with less than 600,000 men, for the SAG South had been heavily mauled by the German summer offensive of 1941. The Germans, with two GAG Souths, probably enjoyed a superiority of at least three to one. The second German summer offensive was directed against Stalingrad by GAG South B and toward the Donets Basin and Caucasus Mountains by GAG South A. These two geographic tangents of the German southern offensive were to separate the two GAGs from each other. GAG South B pushed on toward Stalingrad while GAG South A captured the Donets Basin and raced to the Caucasus Mountains. The Russians, having planned a summer offensive utilizing Russian superiority in the central front, were forced to suspend the offensive and move two SAGs from the central front to behind Stalingrad to await the German arrival. Another SAG South was formed from Soviet reserves guarding the Persian frontier. The Stalingrad probe of GAG South B halted due to the equalization of manpower on the front line. GAG South A was also halted by the newly created SAG South Caucasus.

The Soviet southern autumn offensive of 1942 utilized the three SAGs around Stalingrad. This second Russian offensive began in November, 1942, with a ratio of three SAGs to GAG South B. In this action, GAG South B was surrounded and then almost completely destroyed. GAG South A remained the only German army in the south. Overextended, GAG South A retreated in order, as one SAG faced its lines. Later GAG South A regrouped and faced the four SAGs South.

In the summer of 1943, the battlefield consisted of the basic GAG North, Center, and South. The Soviets, full mobilized, assigned two SAGs to the Leningrad front, four SAGs to the central front, and four SAGs to the southern front. Where the Soviets enjoyed a superiority of over three to one, the Germans were pushed back. Only around the Leningrad front were the Germans able to maintain their defensive line, although the siege of Leningrad was effectively broken. After 1943, the Germans never again attained numerical superiority and their offensive capability was thus blunted. Russian superiority grew during 1943, and the Germans retreated slowly under mounting Soviet pressure.

In 1944 the Russians added a third army group to the northern front, giving them an offensive superiority on all fronts. A quick calculation of all fronts showed 11 SAGs totalling 6,600,000 men. Against them were 1,800,000 German and Axis soldiers divided into three army groups. SAG North drove the German besiegers of Leningrad back to Prussia. SAG Center raced to the outskirts of Warsaw, and SAG South reconquered all German-held Russian territory in the Ukraine, entering Romania, Bulgaria, and Hungary.

In the autumn and winter of 1944–45, the Russians refitted for the last phase of the war—the fourth and final Soviet offensive. The burden of the offensive, which began on January 19, 1945, was on SAG Center. GAG North was cut off by the sweep of the SAG Center to the Baltic. GAG North, surrounded by the Russians, was then destroyed by the SAG North.

SAG Center moved on Berlin, destroying GAG Center, which had been reinforced by SS units. SAG South, with the aid of partisan units including the 250,000 partisans of Tito, captured Prague, Budapest, and Vienna, completing the destruction of GAG South. On May 8, 1945, Germany surrendered and the Great Patriotic War ended.

The above is a simplified version of the war in Russia, attempting to show the dynamics of the large battlefield on which the war was fought. This description can now be augmented by a description of the specific part played by the Siberian Army in the war, to demonstrate the Siberian Army's claim to the words "Special Force" in the Soviet Union, for they were at Stalingrad, at Moscow, and on the road in the center of Berlin.

The German offensive on the road to Moscow was spearheaded by two German panzer armies of GAG Center. This opening offensive faltered, according to various sources, due to autumn mud, to Russian "scorched-earth" policies, to an early harsh winter, to insufficiently clothed soldiers, to lack of lubrication and gas for winter war, and to a myriad of other excuses to cover a failure. Perhaps the failure actually lay in the offensive military doctrine of the Germans contrasted to the Red Army doctrine of retreat and defense-in-depth, in the tradition of Clausewitz, Bleucher, and Shaposhnikov.

The most successful German maneuver was the launching of a pincer movement on a wide front by two panzer armies which would meet and surround the trapped Russian forces. Moving on the inner wall of the great armored trap were regular infantry armies. The German infantry armies, meeting within the armored wall created by the panzer armies, captured up to 600,000 Russians, according to the Germans, in various offensives. More often than not, however, the German infantry army, closing the trap too slowly, left great porous areas between the armored units, through which the retreating Soviet forces escaped. This form of war is the blitzkrieg and kept the Russians off balance until November, 1941.

Hitler had previously informed his military that the Soviets planned to attack Germany. On crossing the Bug River on June 22, 1941, the German generals found no signs of any Soviet offensive preparations. In fact, the Soviets simply retreated. Russian strategy was at all times the classic measures of defense as advocated by Clausewitz. The Soviets allowed the retreat to Moscow to stretch the enemy's communication lines, to allow time to begin a popular people's war, to allow small offensives to unhinge the enemy offensive, and to bring up troops first to equalize manpower and then to achieve the superiority in manpower to strike back. A portion of the retreating Soviet Army was under the direction of Bleucher's pupil Konev.

Between Smolensk and Moscow, Konev had unhinged and slowed the German offensive through appropriate counteroffensives. Konev's retreat to Moscow appeared orderly and avoided entrapment. Although Zhukov led the Soviet armies in front of Moscow, it was Shaposhnikov of Frunze, then a marshal, who directed the planning of the Soviet defense at Moscow. Shaposhnikov remained in Moscow until the German offensive was spent and he was retired for reasons of ill health (or for his criticism of Zhukov).

The previous sections noted that, by November, 1941, the Russians had effectively stabilized the three fronts of the war by mobilizing three SAGs equal in strength to the Germans. In front of Moscow, local German offensives continued to drive back the Russians. This reflected the Russian tactic of building large reserves behind Moscow for a counteroffensive. The Germans were shown only Soviet Worker Brigades, newly formed from the Russian factories. The large reserve army behind the city consisted of two Russian army groups, giving the Soviets a three-to-one numerical superiority at Moscow and resulting in the great Russian winter counteroffensive of 1941.

The winter counteroffensive was actually launched by the Siberian Army. Soviet strategy allowed the SAG Center before Moscow to absorb the blows of the German offensive. This SAG

Center concealed the great buildup behind Moscow of more than 1,000,000 trained winter soldiers. The Soviets, like the Mongols before them, had played a ruse on a grand scale. Playing key roles in the defense of Moscow and in the counteroffensive were Malinovsky, Konev, and Rokossovsky, who each led armies of 100,000 men.

The late entry of the Siberian Army into the European theater was dictated by suspected Japanese military ambitions in the Far East. When the Germans invaded in 1941, the Far Eastern Army became fully mobilized to await a Japanese attack. When the Japanese offensive did not develop, units of the Siberian Army were shifted to Moscow. By September, 1941, an excellent Far Eastern network of Soviet spies advised Stalin that Japan would attack the United States and the United Kingdom. Supporting this view was the fact that the Japanese signed a nonaggression pact with Stalin in 1941. This pact perhaps reflected the Japanese experience with the Siberian Army in 1938-39. It allowed the Japanese to turn their troops freely to Southeastern Asia and the economic advantages of that area. Over 1,000,000 men moved toward Moscow on the Trans-Siberian Railway while a large Siberian Army Group remained in Siberia in case of difficulties. Originally in front of Moscow, Marshal Semyon Timoshenko attempted to stem the German advance. However, he could not successfully maneuver large numbers of troops, and he was succeeded by Zhukov. Zhukov, with his background of work with the Siberian troops, was then able to utilize them in the battle for Moscow. In December, 1941, the Soviet armies struck out against the German offensive, unhinged it, and rolled the Germans back more than 200 miles. The Russian winter offensive, undertaken by the Siberians who were well accustomed to and well dressed for the climate, took the Germans by surprise. The Germans were never again to attack frontally at Moscow.

The victory won at Moscow buoyed the spirits of other Russian fighting units, and the harsh winter months of February and March, 1942, brought the fighting of the first year of the war to an end.

Among the Soviet generals at Moscow grew certain antagonisms against Zhukov. Rokossovsky and Konev, holding a defensive posture before Moscow with no Siberian soldiers, were hard pressed and in need of reserves prior to the counteroffensive. Zhukov's failure to reach his commanders earlier than December apparently led to antagonisms when Zhukov claimed all the glory for Moscow. The excellent defensive maneuvers of the front-line commanders did not receive publicity commensurate with their actions. Bulganin and Khrushchev, two commissars who worked well with the Siberian Army generals were also at Moscow.

In 1942 the German war machine was still active. Its resources for an all-out offensive from the Baltic to the Black Sea were limited. Therefore, the Germans chose to concentrate manpower in a two-pronged offensive against Stalingrad and the oilfields between Rostov and the Caucasus Mountains. German numerical superiority was bolstered by legions of Spanish, Italian, French, Hungarian, and Romanian troops in addition to newly raised German armies. The Germans faced a badly mauled SAG South, which had previously been beaten around Kharkhov.

In 1942 the Soviets had anticipated launching an offensive against GAG Center. Consequently, only a small Siberian Army unit was sent to the southern armies. When the German southern offensive began, the Russians utilized ruse and retreat before the onrushing German armies. Minor parries were utilized by the Soviets to unhinge and slow the German advance as well as to separate these GAGs so they could not support each other.

German intelligence reported that the only army faced by the Germans was the 62nd Siberian Army. This army continued to lure GAG South B to Stalingrad where the 62nd Siberian Army, its units still intact, was able to defend the city. The story of the heroic Russian defense of the city of Stalingrad, only yards from the river, was the story of the 62nd Siberian Army and General Vasily Chuikov, who had just returned from being an advisor to Chiang Kai-shek in Chunking.

While the 62nd Siberian Army slowed the advance of the German armies, two Siberian Army groups were transferred to

Stalingrad from Moscow. These units, as well as other army replacements, were brought north and south of the city of Stalingrad, waiting across the river for the attack. As at Moscow, the Russian armies committed to the fight were smaller than the veteran units waiting behind the lines until the German battle lines had been stretched as far as the Germans dared. Originally, Marshal Timoshenko commanded SAG South, but he was again replaced by Zhukov. Rokossovsky felt that Zhukov had planned to use the same offensive tactics as at Moscow. Rokossovsky called for tactical changes because similar units and commanders were placed as they had been at Moscow. Khrushchev, the political commissar at Stalingrad, was instrumental in having Rokossovsky and Zhukov settle their differences, and Rokossovsky's final troop movements and deployments gained for him a worldwide reputation. Under Zhukov, the counteroffensive at Stalingrad was launched in November, 1942. North of the city, the German lines, filled by Romanian and Italian troops, were crushed by SAG Konev. The surrounding and destruction of GAG South B in Stalingrad had begun. To complete this destruction, the tank armies of Rokossovsky were used. Swift attacks across the Volga, utilizing underwater bridges, allowed the tank units to walk on water. Rokossovsky's units relieved the garrison in the city, allowing Malinovsky's southern portion of the encirclement to sweep out and finally link up with the northern panzer movement. GAG South B became, first, low on supplies, then further away from reinforcements, and finally surrendered in February, 1943.

The remaining GAG South A in the Caucasus and Donets Basin retreated rapidly as their northern supporting GAG South B was destroyed. Units from GAG South A under General Von Mannstein raced to relieve the surrounded GAG at Stalingrad. The Mannstein offensive failed against the superior army of Malinovsky. This action proved to be the last German attempt to relieve the Stalingrad perimeter. When GAG South A had advanced in the summer of 1942, a recently organized Soviet Army Group retreated into the heart of the Caucasus Mountains. With the destruction of the Germans at Stalingrad, the tide turned, and the three SAGs from Stalingrad joined SAG Caucasus. The

Germans retreated rapidly and, under the direction of Von Manstein, contracted and straightened their defensive line. The three SAGs at Stalingrad each contained large numbers of Siberian Army soldiers. A fourth Siberian Army group was formed north of Stalingrad in preparation for further advances. The leaders of these army groups at Stalingrad and the newly formed army group north of Stalingrad were Zhukov, Konev, Rokossovsky, and Malinovsky. Battle maps listed other officers such as General Sokolovsky heading Zhukov's army group. The key to Zhukov's effective control of an army group was his assumption of complete command whenever a major offensive occurred in his sector. Under these leaders the future victories of the war were won. This leadership team included in its ranks Nikita Khrushchev who, as a member of the Politburo, was assigned as political commissar with the armies in the Ukraine, and General Ivan Serov, who led all NKVD troops in the Ukraine. Khrushchev at Stalingrad had come to act as Stalin's mediator and spokesman for the army leaders.

The successful Soviet winter offensive of 1943 in the Stalingrad sector drove the Germans back to the line which marked the gains of the first German offensive of 1941 on the southern front. The Soviets maintained the gains of the Russian winter offensives of 1941 and 1942. The key to understanding the importance of the Soviet victories to the end of the war was found by watching the movement of the four army groups led by the Siberian Army marshals and Zhukov. SAG Rokossovsky was placed on the northern wing, SAG Konev and SAG Zhukov were in the center, and SAG Malinovsky was on the southern wing. These army groups ranged along the central and southern fronts of Russia. Tactically each army group launched alternating offensive actions, keeping the Germans unbalanced and maintaining the initiative. Lull periods for each army group allowed them time for refitting prior to offensive action.

The winter of 1943-44 allowed time for the victorious Soviet armies to modernize at Stalingrad and in the Ukraine. In the spring and summer of 1944, SAG Malinovsky began an offensive push to the Romanian border. This action was stymied by the placement of veteran German divisions, drawn from other fronts, to the southern front. With the weakening of the other German fronts, SAG Rokossovsky was able to drive 400 miles in eighteen days to the outskirts of Warsaw. SAG Konev and SAG Zhukov then began, in alternating pushes, to mop up the German troops remaining in the regions between Warsaw and Romania.

The German divisions which were pulled out of the line to stop the wedge driven by the Siberian Army groups thus allowed other Red Army groups to reclaim the Ukraine and the Crimea, as well as to break effectively the siege of Leningrad. Spearheaded by SAG Rokossovsky, the Soviets were able to begin the reconquest of the Baltic States.

In the winter of 1944-45, the Soviets massed eleven SAGs along the battle line which stretched from the Baltic to the Balkans. Over seven million men poised for the final push. However, only four SAGs did the major share of the fighting, leaving the others for clean-up operations, bypassing large pockets of German troops in the offensives led by Zhukov, Konev, Rokossovsky, and Malinovsky.

The Soviet winter offensive of 1944–45 was broken into four major thrusts. SAG Rokossovsky and SAG Zhukov drove into Berlin after taking Warsaw. SAG Konev feinted for Berlin and drove into southeastern Germany and then into Czechoslovakia. SAG Malinovsky, involved in the fighting for Budapest when the offensive opened, drove for Vienna after the successive conquests of Budapest and Belgrade. Before the Soviet offensive began on January 18, 1945, General Ghelen, German chief of intelligence eastern front, reported to Guderian that the Russians enjoyed a superiority of eleven to one in infantry, seven to one in tanks, and twenty to one in artillery and planes. Certainly the four SAGs involved in the fighting enjoyed more than a three-to-one manpower superiority as well as air control on the drive to Berlin.

Another advantage was established when SAG Rokossovsky broke through to the Baltic, splitting GAG North from GAG Center. Cut-off GAG North contained twenty veteran divisions. The task of mopping up GAG North was left to other Soviet soldiers. SAG Rokossovsky turned toward Berlin. SAG Konev rolled over the Germans and, after pretending to take a southern approach to Berlin, drove through Saxony and into Prague, Czechoslovakia. Berlin, defended by German SS units, fell in late April and its fall was climaxed by Hitler's suicide. Oriental divisions, members of the 62nd Siberian Army (renamed the 18th Guards Army under Chuikov), figured heavily in the attack on Berlin and were considered by the Germans to be the most dangerous troops the Russians had. When the war ended, the banners of the Siberian armies flew over five capitals—Berlin, Prague, Vienna, Warsaw, and Budapest. To each marshal was then accorded the prize of a European capital. Although Belgrade was also taken by the Siberian armies, the majority of the fighting had been done by Tito's partisan army.

This was a simplified version of World War II in Russia, expanded to show the specific roles of the elite Siberian Army units and the officers associated with these units. Not all soldiers in the four Soviet Army Groups were Siberians, but the assault troops of the Soviet armies were Orientals.

Lack of accurate information on the Soviet war effort allowed many myths and questions to arise which remain unanswered. With the war in Europe ended, the Allied Western armies pondered the relative strength of the Soviet juggernaut that had swept over Eastern Europe. The German soldiers told of the weakness and ineffectiveness of the Russian fighting soldier. The German soldier felt that one German division could defeat five or more Russian divisions. This may have been true prior to October, 1941, but after that time the battle map showed a different story.

Another question raised concerning the war was the effectiveness of the blitzkrieg. Shortly after the war had begun, both the British and the Russian commanders had allowed the tank units to pass through the lines during a blitzkrieg attack. Antitank and tank units would then engage each other in the rear of the front lines. At the same time the British and Soviet front lines would re-form to await the German infantry, upon which large losses were then inflicted by Allied commanders, who did not worry about the panzer units in their rear, as at Kursk-Orel in 1943. Field Marshal Bernard Montgomery in Egypt and Siberian Army commanders were masters of this art of defense. Russian tactics modified the German blitzkrieg by permitting the Soviet tanks to advance only as fast as the Soviet infantry units. In this way, an outside and inside perimeter would be erected simultaneously around surrounded German units. This coordination of tank and infantry units was the basis for the fame of Rokossovsky. This tactic could be used successfully by the Soviets because the Siberian soldier was able to march forty or more miles a day, infiltrating the German lines before the tanks attacked.

Others have mused retrospectively that if the Allied Western armies had continued to fight the Russians across the Elbe River into Russia, the weak Russian army would have been destroyed, preventing future conflict. The battle map supports the thesis that Stalin may have been anticipating such an action from the Western powers or he may have intended a counteroffensive of his own, depending on the outcome of postwar negotiations. In May, 1945, five Allied army groups faced four battle proven SAGs. These SAGs were the soldiers of the Siberian Army, the best fighting units of the Russians. However, relatively unknown behind the front lines were seven other SAGs, biding their time mopping up in the Baltic and Balkan areas. In fact, the Soviets maintained in Russia a backup reserve force capable of being utilized in an all-out war.

In total, there were 6,600,000 front line effectives and more than half that number in Russia in reserve army groups. Some reports state that 15 million Russians were under arms. The five Western Allied army groups totalled three million men. In addition to the Soviet soldiers, the Allies faced the Communist-oriented partisans of Yugoslavia, Greece, Albania, Poland, Romania, and Hungary, all under Soviet control. Should an Allied advance from the west have been undertaken, the Allied armies could easily have been crushed by the Soviet troops on the defensive. Stalin was able to utilize two of these Siberian Army groups against Japan. Apparently the Soviet generals must have been impressed by the lasting fighting qualities of these elite troops and they were thus maintained on a war footing.

By the end of the war, Russian-built artillery and tanks ranked in quantity and quality with the finest in the world. American Lend-Lease tanks supplied to Russia did not match the 1941 model T-34 tank or the successor Stalin tanks. The Stalin Organ, an artillery piece, manufactured and used in 1941, was not utilized by the Americans until 1943. Much American military hardware supplied as Lend-Lease was wasted in Russia, as most Russian soldiers could not master the mechanics of American equipment. Soviet equipment continued to be built more simply and at a fraction of the cost of American equipment. The lessons of previous wars had taught Russia that she must build most of her own military equipment if she were to fight from the Bug to Berlin.

It was true that American and British fighter planes were better in action against the German fighters than were the Soviet airplanes. However, Russian planes were built to be coordinated with the infantry and to increase the Soviet firepower in any ground action. The Soviet planes, armed with cannon rather than machine guns, were built to fly in the worst weather conditions. During the Battle of the Bulge, the typical Soviet fighter would have been able to maintain Allied air superiority during the wintry days that grounded all Axis and Allied air units.

In reappraising the Soviet-German war, the Soviet Union apparently was able to build and equip fighting units that were comparable to the finest fighting units in the world at that time. When the war ended in 1945, the Western Powers demobilized, while the Soviets maintained their best fighting units for future use.

STALIN'S POSTWAR MANEUVERS IN ASIA AND EUROPE

The Soviet Far Eastern (Siberian) Army had guarded the long Sino-Soviet frontiers from Japanese attack during the war. From 1941 to 1944, Siberian Army officers maintained and staffed an enlarged Outer Mongolian fighting force. In addition, men of the Siberian Army entered the Sinkiang Province in Northwestern China. This area, under nominal control from Chungking, was the transportation route for Sino-Soviet trade during the war. Before the Sovietization of Sinkiang Province had become a fact, the conference table at Yalta in February, 1945, decided on a different fate for Soviet ambitions in Asia. Due to American and British fears of heavy casualties in an invasion of the Japanese homeland, Russia was asked for further contributions to the war effort for which she was to receive new territorial concessions and spheres of influence in Asia. Rather than Sinkiang Province, the Soviets were to gain Manchuria and North Korea after the war.

Estimates that over 1,000,000 Allied soldiers would be killed or wounded in an invasion of Japan weighed heavily on the minds of General George C. Marshall and other American military planners. By bringing the Soviets into the war, they hoped these casualty figures could be reduced. In 1945, there were still large, as yet unbeaten, Japanese armies in Manchuria, China, and Southeastern Asia which perhaps could have reinforced the home islands. As late as 1944 these armies had launched a successful offensive against Chinese troops and American-built B-29 bases in China. After the Japanese destroyed most of these air bases, they were as close to Chungking as two hundred miles. American army planners believed that the Japanese troops in China were veteran units which remained undefeated in war and totalled more than one million soldiers, an imposing figure.

In February, 1945, at the time of the Yalta Conference, the atomic bomb had not yet been proven in the war as a military factor. By March, 1945, the atomic bomb had been exploded at Alamogordo, New Mexico. In total, only two bombs were in production for 1945. When Roosevelt died in April, 1945, few Americans knew of the bomb's potential. When President Harry Truman went to Potsdam, he did not appear to realize that Japan could be brought to her feet by the two remaining atomic bombs. Roosevelt and later Truman did exact guarantees from the Soviets concerning the evacuation of Sinkiang and the Soviet maintenance of the Chiang Kai-shek regime in China in return for Soviet future rights to Port Arthur, Manchuria, and North Korea.

To destroy the Japanese forces in Manchuria, the Siberian Army returned to Siberia from Europe. They moved across the steppes and then rested to plan for the next offensive action. Over one million men returned to the Manchurian-Outer Mongolian border. For Malinovsky and other Siberian soldiers, this was a return match for the Red Army that had fought the Japanese in 1918 and 1939. In the summer of 1945, the battle order for the conquest of Manchuria showed three Soviet Army Groups, originally led by Marshal Meretskov and Purkaev in Siberia and Malinovsky in Outer Mongolia, with overall leadership assigned to Marshal Vasilevsky, a Stalinist general. Malinovsky's importance in this campaign is shown by his being named to replace Vasilevsky as overall commander of the Far Eastern armies at the end of the Japanese war.

The Soviet Summer Asian Offensive began, after months of extensive preparations, on August 8, 1945. The victorious Siberian armies poured down from the Maritime Provinces and from Outer Mongolia, through to the boot of Korea, to destroy the Japanese. At the same time the American atomic bomb was dropped. The bombing of Hiroshima on August 6, 1945, the bombing of Nagasaki soon after, with the destruction of many civilians, contributed to the immobilization of about 1,000,000 Japanese troops by the Soviets.

A Soviet government, supposedly paralyzed by the Soviet-German war, was able to launch more than one million fighting troops in an offensive action against Japan. Fortunately for the Soviets, most of the Japanese troops had not seen action since 1942, and many veteran troops had been secretly transported to the Pacific Theater to fight the Americans.

At the end of the war Stalin kept the Yalta agreement by ending Soviet influence in Sinkiang Province. In Manchuria Soviet influence and interaction with the Chinese Nationalists and Communists were more ambivalent than purposeful. This period could be compared to 1927 in China when Soviet foreign policy had become confused between the ideals of Marxism and the practicalities of Chinese political life. The Soviets under Malinovsky proceeded to strip the Japanese Manchurian industries, leaving neither of the contending Chinese parties a base for future industrial production. Malinovsky also officially stated the Soviet position of refusing any arms to the Chinese Communists. However, Mao Tse-tung did order 50,000 men from the Communist Eighth Route Army under Lin Piao into Manchuria. The Chinese Communists then took by force Japanese arms and ammunition and obstructed the entry of Nationalist troops into Manchuria. Mao Tse-tung, when asked where he had gained his weapons for the conquest of China, answered not too cryptically, "from London and Washington arsenals." In short, most of Mao's weapons arrived as gifts from Chiang's troops, rather than from the Japanese or the Soviets.

Stalin's dislike of Mao Tse-tung was personal as well as a result of Mao's successful rural revolution, in contrast to the failure of Stalin's urban basis for a revolution in China. Mao's insistence on rural support proved to be the key to the Communist success in China. Stalin's enmity to Mao lasted through 1950 when a Sino-Soviet agreement set forth Soviet and Chinese spheres of influence. Only then did Soviet economic and military aid return to Communist China. It was in 1950 and 1951 that the first Chinese-flown but Russian-built MIGs appeared in the skies over Korea as a direct result of this belated military assistance.

Malinovsky and his Siberian legions departed from Manchuria in 1946 and from North Korea in 1948. In Siberia from 1945 to 1955, Malinovsky maintained the fighting spirit of the Far Eastern Army, remodeling and maintaining the armies of the satellite buffer states. After the world war ended, Malinovsky placed former Siberian Army soldiers in power in North Korea. The president of North Korea was Kim Il-sung, a former Siberian Army colonel who had fought in Stalingrad. Kim Il-sung's support rested mainly on the regiments of North Korean soldiers who had returned from the Siberian Army campaigns in Europe. This North Korean Army had done well against the South Korean Army in 1950, but against the stronger American forces they had fallen back to the Yalu River. With the defeat of the North Korean Army in 1950, Lin Piao was able to reestablish the status quo by leading the Chinese Communist armies against the United

Nations forces. Because of the 1950 Sino-Soviet agreement the Russians kept North Korea within their sphere of influence and, even though the Chinese drove the United Nations out of North Korea by force of arms, Kim Il-sung remained president of North Korea. Many Chinese-oriented North Koreans were then executed in 1953-54, and only Russian-oriented North Koreans have remained in power. These Sino-Soviet interactions in Korea and earlier in Manchuria explain why the Chinese contemptuously speak of the Russians as "big brothers."

Other Siberian Army generals also spent their time training and establishing satellite armies after World War II. In the western marches of the Soviet Empire Konev organized the army of Hungary in 1945 and the army of East Germany in 1946. He also reorganized the Czechoslovakian army in 1951. For his role in the satellites, Konev was named the overall head of all the forces of the satellite nations by 1955. Rokossovsky was also busy during this period, training a Polish army. As Polish minister of defense and Konev's deputy as leader of the Warsaw Pact nations' armed forces. Rokossovsky also maintained the Soviet grip over the satellite forces. This is contrasted with the actions in Yugoslavia in 1948 and Albania in 1961 where non-Siberian-advised armies were able to break completely from Russian rule.

The maintenance of the satellite armies under the direction of Bleucher's pupils protected both the eastern and the western marches of the Soviet Empire. An officer corps, trained in a single tradition, was protecting the borders of the Soviet Union.

The Soviet Army, and especially the Siberian Army, has reequipped itself in five-year modernization cycles repeatedly since 1945. This has meant that the latest tanks, modernized rifles, increased artillery firepower, the newest in ICBMs and other types of rocketry, a large number of helicopters, and a high degree of mechanization have been added to all the Soviet armies. The addition of enlarged airborne contingents to this army has also occurred. Their transport planes are presently used by the civilian Russian passenger airline service, Aeroflot. The ease with which the Tu 104 and the Tu 114 long-distance passenger turboprops and jets can be adapted to military purposes has not gone unnoticed. American tourists have noticed the abundance of Soviet turboprops and jets even in the most distant points in Siberia. The Siberian Army also undertook large scale amphibious training exercises. These training exercises were discovered when one of the Soviet landing craft was found 1,000 miles off course in the Pacific Ocean. These amphibious training exercises, along with the addition of airborne units, have made the Siberian Army today broader in tactical scope than the American Marines. There is nothing new in the Soviet use of airborne or amphibious troops. Soviet use of parachute troops dates back prior to World War II, when Russia boasted of the largest airborne force in the world. Soviet parachutists were used only in minor military airborne jumps in World War II, as the German juggernaut pushed farther back into Russia. Parachute units were instead committed to the infantry and they passed unnoticed. Soviet utilization of amphibious landings dates back to the Finnish War and to Soviet attempts to resupply and retake the Crimea in 1942–43.

The victories of the Siberian Army as a source of the stability of the Soviet state and the consummation of the Kremlin's policies have been described to this point. Since 1953, the Siberian Army and its leaders have played a more vital role in maintaining political stability in Russia. The next chapters will describe the transition of the Siberian Army from the protector of the borders of the empire to the seat of power in the Kremlin.

THE ENDING OF THE STALIN ERA

Stalin attempted successfully after World War II to consolidate his position as leader of the Soviet Union by isolating the position and power of each potential rival. In this way Stalin was able to remain in complete control of the Soviet Union until his death. The war had brought forth strong claimants for the right of succeeding Stalin. He watched these claimants suspiciously, feeling they might not wait until he died. The claimants arose from the Secret Police in the person of Beria; from the technocrats and the Communist party, in Malenkov, Zhdanov, and Khrushchev;

from the Foreign Ministry, in Molotov; and from the Soviet Army, in the victorious marshals who had led the Siberian Army.

Beria's power rested upon the Secret Police (NKVD), the foreign and domestic spy network, and the Soviet atomic energy program. The army of the Secret Police was used to maintain surveillance over the forced labor, which totalled one million men, employed in rebuilding basic industries. The NKVD also maintained intensive domestic surveillance systems, reaching from the collective farms to the Politburo. The triumphs of Beria included maintaining German and Soviet atomic scientists who helped develop the Soviet atomic bomb in 1949 and a true hydrogen bomb in 1952. The Russian hydrogen bomb preceded its American counterpart by six months. The Western press considered Beria a faithful follower of Stalin after the purges in the 1930s, yet Stalin maintained a Supra-Secret Police to control Beria. This unit, led by trusted generals under Stalin's personal direction, bypassed Beria while checking the function of the NKVD. The Supra-Secret Police unit was led by General Poskrabytchev.

The Communist party was the second source of powerful leaders and potential rivals. The power of Malenkov or Khrushchev was based on their control of party membership. Malenkov used his position in Moscow to place his own supporters in the Moscow party apparatus and in the Leningrad party apparatus. Khrushchev, who had been a Moscow party functionary during the late 1930s, controlled a few Muscovite votes in addition to the Ukrainian party apparatus. The war years had seen Khrushchev serving as reorganizer for reconquered Soviet territory in the Ukraine. Men loyal to him were placed in all levels of the Ukrainian party apparatus. At the same time, Khrushchev built up personal friendships with the Siberian Army generals and with Marshal Zhukov. In addition, he was able to appoint men like Leonid Brezhnev to be political commissars of the Siberian Army troops fighting in the Ukraine. Khrushchev also had made the acquaintance of members of the NKVD who, like General Serov, were to prove useful to him later.

Zhdanov, a powerful Communist party leader after World

War II, seemed to be Stalin's heir apparent. However, when Zhdanov died in 1948, his place was taken by Malenkov.

Jockeying for the control of power of the Communist party and its many technocrats first saw Malenkov victorious over his many rivals. This situation changed in the late 1940s. At that time Khrushchev returned to Moscow full-time, and a Khrushchev supporter was sent to replace Malenkov's man in Leningrad. This appointment of Aleksei Kosygin later assured Khrushchev's rise to power, but in the late 1940s it served to diminish Malenkov's stature as heir to Stalin.

The Foreign Ministry, represented by Molotov, had no army and was closely watched by the NKVD. Thus it was kept too far from the seat of power to lay claim to the rule of the Soviet lands.

Stalin's strongest rivals, viewed at the end of the war, were the army marshals. These leaders were supported by whole army groups. Zhukov, Konev, Malinovsky, and Rokossovsky were cited among the most successful military leaders in the Soviet Victory Orders of the Day in 1945. Zhukov, the most popular Russian military leader, was compared with America's Eisenhower.

In 1945 the military leaders had split into two camps. Non-Siberian Army front-line marshals, such as Sokolovsky, formed the right wing of the army, boasting of their role in the war and attempting to downgrade the political commissar system in the army. The left wing of the marshals consisted of the Siberian Army generals and their staff, consisting of men such as Grechko, Chuikov, and Malinin. The Siberian Army clique, led by Konev, Malinovsky, and Rokossovsky, jealously watched Zhukov's rise to popularity, believing that his role in the war left much to be desired. Stalin was effectively able to utilize the army split to downgrade Zhukov in 1946 and to replace him with Konev. The popularity that Zhukov commanded led to his political resurrection in 1953.

Stalin probably entertained the idea of destroying the Siberian officer clique in light of any impending power struggle in postwar Moscow. The decision not to destroy these officers was based on Stalin's memories of the early days of the German onslaught into Russia. At that time a decimated post-purge officer corps was unable to put up effective resistance against Hitler's armies. Stalin would not allow the Siberian Army clique to be concentrated in Moscow where the leaders could possibly rival him. Instead, Stalin separated these officers from each other, at the same time stressing via propaganda his own role in the victory over Germany. In 1946, Konev was appointed commander in chief of the Soviet armies, but the Siberian Army, upon which his power rested, was moved 6,000 miles away and was placed first under a Stalinist officer, Vasilevsky, and then under Malinovsky when Stalin's political horizons looked clearer. Rokossovsky was moved from Moscow to his birthplace in Poland where he ruled as defense minister and member of the Polish Politburo. Konev was later moved to Germany and Czechoslovakia. Stalin demoted Zhukov, first to the Odessa Military District and then to the Urals. The commands in Warsaw, in Prague, and in Siberia were far away from both Moscow and the center of power.

Stalin maintained control of these officers through political commissars, through strict NKVD surveillance, through fear of purge and through the mechanics of distance. Of the political leaders left in Moscow, only Khrushchev of the Soviet Politburo had worked well with the Siberian Army clique both in Moscow and in Stalingrad. Khrushchev's success as political commissar had been his ability to remain in the background, allowing the military to take full glory for the victories in the Ukraine. This glory was later accredited by Stalin to himself. The three war years in which Khrushchev worked with Zhukov and the Siberian Army clique are the key to understanding the directions taken in the power struggle upon Stalin's death.

Because of Stalin's policy of isolating the various claimants to his power, his potential successors needed time to consolidate their positions after his death. Beria, Molotov, and Malenkov at first linked forces. Beria was the most important member of the original triumvirate because his NKVD army provided the security needed during the transition period. Molotov maintained Soviet foreign policy, while Malenkov dealt with internal affairs. Molotov and Malenkov especially needed Beria to destroy the last vestige of Stalin's personal power, the Supra-Secret Police. Its members, who could have been used to strike down the Politburo, were all executed. Stalin's personal purgers were dead and could no longer be used by any of the rival claimants to Stalin's powers. Beria was left in complete control of the country's internal security and thus the most powerful member of the triumvirate. This brought about a realignment of the leaders of the various factions.

Malenkov and Molotov attempted immediately to utilize the power of the army to control and then destroy Beria. The army's price for supporting Malenkov and Molotov was that their most trusted man, Nikita Khrushchev, be named head of the Communist party. Malenkov was to remain as premier of the Soviet Union. For the first time since World War II, the army marshals were able to communicate more freely and to exert their influence. Both the left- and right-wing marshals forgot their grievances to unite behind Zhukov. The army marshals hoped to avoid both a repetition of the 1936-38 purges and a left-versus-right struggle which could allow a third party to come to power. By using Zhukov's prestige as well as their newfound unity, the army marshals avoided extinction. It was hoped that Zhukov would promote popular support for the government through his own popular support among the people, thus averting open rebellion.

Beria made an attempt at gaining popular support through propaganda painting a liberal picture of himself. The other members of the Politburo, fearing Beria's assumption of control, realized that the awesome power of the Secret Police had to be neutralized before Beria could be destroyed. The seizure of Beria's power had to be swift, as a full-scale civil war would lead not only to Beria's downfall but perhaps to the downfall of the .party itself. The plot to unseat Beria was months in planning and involved making large-scale maneuvers around the major posts of the NKVD at the same time Beria was to be killed. Coordinating this putsch was Konev, and the single most important task, that of assassinating Beria, fell to Marshal Maslenniko. In 1953, Maslenniko was the military commandant of the Moscow Military District. Maslenniko's men surrounded the NKVD headquarters in Moscow, at the same time that Beria was called to a meeting of the Politburo. At this meeting Beria was accused of treason. In short time a tribunal led by Konev sentenced Beria to death. To assure army control of the NKVD, General Ivan Serov was appointed head of the organization. General Serov, as previously mentioned, was an NKVD general who had served with the Siberian Army generals and Khrushchev in the Ukraine and was apparently trusted by all the parties involved. This trust probably came as a result of Serov's using NKVD troops in the front lines during battle actions rather than as reserve troops who shot down any retreating Russian soldiers. In 1953 Serov was the only high-ranking NKVD leader to survive the Beria purge. General Serov was later replaced by a civilian as head of the NKVD after the Secret Police had lost all their power and all the military units had been semi-incorporated into the army.

The Soviet marshals faced only Molotov and Malenkov as the steppingstones to complete power. Malenkov and Molotov had created support for themselves, both within the Communist party and among the many bureaucrats in the industries. The military demanded top priority to maintain a strong military posture for the continued Soviet-Western cold war. Zhukov and the Siberian Army marshals looked for the continued maintenance of heavy industries and the building of a transportation network to support the complexities of modern warfare. Since the investments in complicated armaments had become continually greater, and since the military demands for the replacement of obsolete weapons had become more persistent, the new Soviet government was committed to maintaining Stalin's economic system. Malenkov, in a bid for popular support and for Communist party leadership, took a stand for increased expenditures on consumer goods. This action brought Malenkov into direct conflict with the military. The marshals moved quickly against their former ally and removed him. To disperse potential Malenkov support among the technocrats in industry, Khrushchev and the marshals decentralized the Soviet industrial system. However, the industries which were responsible for military weapons continued to be centralized in Moscow under the watchful eyes of the marshals.

The military was so sure of its firm position in power that

Malenkov was allowed to live in exile beyond the Urals, under observation of the Siberian Army groups. Khrushchev was able to leave the Soviet Union on extended visits to non-Communist countries. Zhukov and the Siberian Army marshals felt they could maintain a stable state in his absence.

The Khrushchev era of Soviet politics had begun in 1955, although it could perhaps be called the era of the Siberian Army marshals. Their influence became paramount in 1957 when their rise to complete power coincided with Zhukov's fall from leadership. From 1953 to 1957, Zhukov had been minister of defense and, because of his popularity, had been added to the Politburo as a candidate member. By 1955 Malinovsky was first deputy defense minister, after having completed a ten-year tour of duty with the Siberian Army in Asia. Konev returned to Moscow as the newly appointed head of the Warsaw Pact nations and in 1955 Rokossovsky was in Poland as minister of defense and as Konev's deputy. Among these four men was divided the actual control of the armed forces of the Soviet Union and through them the new leaders of the Kremlin brought the Stalin era to an end.

THE SIBERIAN ARMY TO POWER

From 1953 to 1962 the Soviet Union was ruled through crises and conflicts by the army marshals. Between 1953 and 1957 a *modus vivendi* of the army marshals had created an atmosphere which eased the tensions both for the world at large and in the Kremlin. The delicate balance which existed in Moscow was broken by Zhukov's political failure to preserve the stability of the Soviet empire in 1956 and 1957. Clausewitz taught that an army was the extension of the political needs of a state and that, in the final analysis, a military leader had to be as politically adroit as he had to be militarily adept. Zhukov's political naiveté led to his replacement by Bleucher's politically more adroit pupils.

Satellite rumblings of discontent had begun soon after Stalin's death. Riots had occurred in East Germany in 1953, an uprising Konev was able to suppress without resorting to excessive bloodshed. Later in 1956, a large-scale revolution of Hungarians against the Communist government took place. Many Russian soldiers stationed in Hungary openly refused to fight the revolutionaries.

Feelings of nationalism neutralized the fighting ability of the Hungarian soldiers. In October, 1956, the potential loss of Hungary was a threat to the stability of the Soviet Empire. Various factions of the Soviet Politburo squabbled over the nature of the action to be taken against Hungary. This led to two weeks of inaction. Before the Soviets decided to act, Marshal Malinovsky had already airlifted his Siberian troops to Romania and the Russo-Hungarian frontier. Zhukov himself was unable to move the Politburo to act. The Anglo-French invasion of the Suez provided an excuse for Soviet intervention in Hungary, and Malinovsky's troops marched. The Siberian troops were quickly able to put down the Hungarian rebellion. Hungarian refugees described Oriental soldiers who, unlike the White Russian soldiers, fought well in the streets of Budapest. The Siberian troops, however, may have been told that the city they were to conquer was Berlin, not Budapest.

Other rebellious stirrings were heard in Poland in 1956. The Polish army, tired of Soviet intervention in Polish politics, had chosen to support a moderate Communist leader, Wladyslaw Gomulka. To satisfy the Poles, Rokossovsky was made the scapegoat. It is not difficult to surmise that Rokossovsky had appealed to Zhukov for military aid to support his isolated position. Instead, Zhukov and Khrushchev came to Warsaw to wave their fingers at Gomulka. Since this was all they were to do, Rokossovsky was forced to leave Poland in disgrace. Zhukov's failure to send aid could be contrasted to Malinovsky's use of troops in Hungary and Konev's use of tanks in East Germany. Rokossovsky's continued hostility and coolness toward Zhukov led to Rokossovsky's demotion from a deputy Soviet minister of defense to a commandant of a military district in 1957, thereby increasing Rokossovsky's distaste for Zhukov.

The anti-party fiasco of 1957 was Zhukov's final blunder. In June, 1957, the discontents of the Politburo had become alarmed at Khrushchev and the Soviet Army policies. They had turned on Khrushchev in particular, repudiating his policies. Even "safe" members of the Politburo such as Shepilov and Nikolai Bulganin, supposedly friendly toward the Siberian Army clique, and Zhukov from the Moscow and Ukrainian days, voted against Khrushchev. Zhukov was apparently taken by surprise again. Other military officers, directed by Malinovsky, Konev, and Rokossovsky, pushed for a meeting of the Central Committee to stall and perhaps save Khrushchev and their Soviet government. The Central Committee of the Communist Party was corraled by the Soviet Army marshals and rushed by transport to Moscow. There, after a stern lecture by the military, defeat was turned into victory and Khrushchev's policies were reaffirmed. Quick and unified military support in the provinces allowed Khrushchev to win his political victory and with it the well-policed exile of the anti-Khrushchev faction. Malenkov went to Siberia and Molotov went to Outer Mongolia, both watched by the Far Eastern Army Command.

In Moscow, Zhukov had failed to prevent the political machinations of the Politburo. Later he tried to claim eminence for saving Khrushchev's role in the party. This was too much for the marshals of the Siberian Army clique and, after Zhukov demoted Rokossovsky, many more Soviet marshals joined the Siberian Army clique to unseat Zhukov. Zhukov learned of his fall and subsequent removal while on a trip to Yugoslavia. Realizing that he had no power, he quietly retired. Bleucher's heirs were firmly in power, and the following years of Khrushchev's reign must be understood in terms of the likes and dislikes of the Siberian Army clique which ruled the Kremlin.

Malinovsky ranked highest in terms of seniority as a military commander of the elite Siberian Army. He thus became minister of defense. Konev, who had served with its legions from 1920 through 1945, was appointed first deputy minister of defense and head of the Warsaw Pact nations' armies. Rokossovsky returned to Moscow first as a deputy minister of defense and then as a military spokesman on the Central Committee. But the lessons of the anti-party crisis taught that many more marshals should sit in the ruling house of the Communist party, to destroy the chances of any further political coups. By 1961 twenty other Soviet marshals and generals had become members of the Central Committee. It was thus unlikely that the Communist party could avoid the likes or dislikes of the Soviet military in power. In 1957, Rokossovsky was the least important of the three top military leaders of the Soviet Union. One suspects that Rokossovsky, the most outspoken of the three marshals, had little of the diplomacy of Konev or Malinovsky. But Rokossovsky's role as the finest Soviet tank and troop commander during the war maintained his voice in the councils of the triumvirate.

One particular dislike of the Siberian Army clique was Marshal Voroshilov. In 1938 Voroshilov had presumably destroyed Bleucher while serving as Stalin's messenger. Without Zhukov to shield him after 1957, Voroshilov was removed as president of the Presidium in partial revenge for the death of Bleucher. Adding insult to injury, Voroshilov, who had taken the salutes of the Red Army, was now refused admission to the May Day proceedings. Voroshilov could now only watch as Bleucher's heirs took the salutes of the Red Army and watched the glory of the Soviet military power pass by.

The hand behind Voroshilov in 1938 also met with insult at the hands of the marshals. Stalin fell in disrepute after the speeches of the Twentieth Party Congress. Stalin's body was removed and placed, unmarked, near the Kremlin Wall. After the Siberian Army triumvirate assumed power, the role of the political commissar was remodeled after the pattern of Khrushchev's relations to the military at Stalingrad. Other political commissars, from political indoctrinators to military thinkers, whom the marshals felt had overstepped their bounds, were also downgraded. Political commissars who had followed Khrushchev's pattern in their relations with the Siberian Army were Demetri Ustinov, Leonid Brezhnev, and Demetri Polyanski. Those political commissars attached to the Siberian Army who followed and supported the marshals' dictates and principles have risen to prominent positions in the Kremlin.

Marshal Malinovsky's ascendency to power was reflected during the Paris Conference in 1960, where pictures of Khrushchev showed a bearlike Malinovsky glowering over the chairman of the Soviet Union. The background events which torpedoed the Paris Conference occurred during the May Day celebration of 1960, when Malinovsky was informed that a U-2 had been brought down by rocket fire. Prior to this incident, Malinovsky had agreed in principle with Khrushchev's policy of attempting to reduce further world tensions. With Khrushchev's successful diplomacy in 1959 at Camp David and across the United States, the Siberian Army marshals had remained quiescent. Khrushchev's policy of reducing world tensions had included the unilateral ending of megaton bomb testing. The U-2 incident brought home to the Siberian Army marshals that Khrushchev's policies had failed and that they would have to assume complete control of political and military policy as set forth in the doctrines of Clausewitz. In Paris Malinovsky proceeded to dictate to Khrushchev a firm foreign policy line toward the Western powers. Khrushchev's voice rang with great bellicosity first in Paris and later at the United Nations. Meanwhile, behind the scenes, Malinovsky, Konev, and Rokossovsky directed the policies of the Soviet Union, providing the glue that has maintained the Soviet empire—the Siberian Army.

Utilizing the spy trial of Gary Powers as a powerful propaganda excuse, the Soviet marshals embarked on further military expenditures. By 1962, these new expenditures had caused a rise in the prices of the basic consumer commodities to provide the necessary increased revenues. The Soviet marshals also felt that the Soviets lagged behind the United States in developing atomic weapons. In late 1961 the series of atomic weaponry tested was used by the Soviets to recover from their feelings of inferiority.

The question frequently arose, after Khrushchev, whom? The nature of the present Soviet power structure appeared to determine that the leaders of the Soviet Army clique would choose and maintain future political leaders. Malinovsky, Konev, and Rokossovsky, behind the scene, would dictate their choice. Prodded to name the man who would succeed Khrushchev, one could suggest a theory and a man. This theory would state that the man to succeed Khrushchev would have to have been connected with the Siberian Army as a political commissar and would have to have been close to Khrushchev. The choice would be a man from the Ukrainian party apparatus. Leonid Brezhnev served as a political commissar of the Siberian armies in the Ukraine and, by 1949, was a member of the Central Committee in the Ukraine. In 1952, Brezhnev followed Khrushchev to Moscow. In 1954 he gained further contact with the Siberian Army clique by becoming coordinating political administrator for the Ministry of Defense in Moscow. After this tour of duty Brezhnev had a meteoric rise. He was to become a member of the ruling Politburo and the President of the Soviet Union. Pictures taken of Brezhnev in 1962 showed him standing next to Khrushchev. Of course, on the other side of Khrushchev stood Malinovsky.

To reemphasize a point, the new government would still be under the military, based upon leadership of the Siberian Army. Malinovsky or Konev could easily have assumed party leadership, although their success at manipulating backstage politics while keeping their names out of the limelight made it unlikely that they would want to be the titular heads of the Soviet Union. It was their control of the Central Committee in Moscow that reduced the chance for any political upheaval upon Khrushchev's succession of power to Brezhnev. The army, strongly entrenched in the Central Committee, would also be able to choose the other members of the Presidium. In this way the machinations of the various Communist party groups in the Soviet Union would remain under the watchful eye of the Siberian Army clique.

The army leadership continued to be represented by Malinovsky and Konev, and they, with Rokossovsky, have already prepared their own heirs. These men are Marshal Chuikov of the 62nd Siberian Army at Stalingrad; Marshal Grechko, who has remained affiliated with Konev; and Marshal Malinin, who is personally tied to Rokossovsky.

If the stability and the succession to power in the Soviet Union have been guaranteed by the strength of the Siberian Army, what policies can be expected to emanate from the Soviet Union? The first conclusion is that the Soviet military posture will continue to be maintained. This involves continuing large expenditures in weapon systems as well as the modernization of the armies. The Soviets will stress the development of antimissile missiles, more sophisticated rocketry, increasing the capabilities of the atom, and increasing the subsurface and surface fleets. The Soviet military will demand better living conditions for their soldiers and will stress heavy industry rather than consumer products. Since the army leaders have remained conscious of the role of the infantry in war, one cannot discount the continued upkeep of large numbers of mobile troops. The upkeep and modernization of the Siberian Army, a conventional force trained in atomic warfare, remains a deterrent to Chinese ambitions toward Southeastern Asia. While the United States has remained preoccupied with a European deterrent force in NATO, the Soviets have probably planned a different form of war. In a war situation they will wait for the United States to commit itself first with the majority of its troops in Europe. After the United States has done this, Soviet submarines will then blockade American and European ports. The Siberian Army will then cross the Bering Straits, a distance of forty miles, or land farther down the long Alaskan or Canadian coastline. Long range helicopters will airlift atomic artillery and fast tanks to the Siberian forces in Alaska and Canada. These troops sweeping down the coast will attempt to destroy American military forces brought against them. Should the American forces fail to halt the Siberian Army, the war could quickly be brought to an end in a nonescalated nonatomic war. This is the meaning of the continued maintenance of a large Siberian Army.

The Soviet Union, to justify her military expenditures, will use as an excuse the continued high American military expenditures. The domestic policy of the Siberian Army clique will continue to sacrifice butter for guns; the foreign policy of the Siberian Army clique will stress disarmament to lull the Western powers.

Other aspects of Soviet policy may also be derived from the specific interests of the Siberian Army clique. Recalling Clausewitz's tenets on war and Russia's historical policy, one military dictum is that maintaining a defensive position has been the finest form of war. Thus, the Soviets will continue to maintain large eastern and western buffer zones and not provoke a war, but rather they will continue their position in the satellites. The Soviet Army believes it has not fought an offensive war since 1945. The Hungarian episode can then be viewed as Soviet determination to keep American armed might as far away as possible from the Soviet lands. This policy is the same as American foreign military policy, which dictated intervention in Lebanon, Cuba, South Vietnam, and Korea.

Soviet flexion of their military muscle will occur when the Soviets feel a definite threat to the maintenance of their defensive posture. One such threat is found in Berlin, where the Soviets will require a solution which neutralizes the position of Berlin in world politics. Since Berlin stands 100 miles within the Soviet territory's defensive perimeter, the future of Berlin will remain foremost in the Soviet military mind as a salient of the West to be blotted out.

If the road to London and Washington is through Africa and Asia, the Soviet policy will continue to stress the wars of national liberation in Africa, Asia, and South America. Malinovsky's behind-the-scenes role would be in building revolutionary armies favorably disposed to the Soviets. In 1962 General Kong Lee, representing the neutralist Laotian Army, visited Moscow. If General Lee maintains his position as head of the Laotian Army through large-scale Soviet military aid, then the United States will face repercussions in Thailand and Burma that will lead to London and Washington.

Early in 1962, Malinovsky visited Morocco to talk with the FLN Algerian leaders. Soon after his visit, Soviet military equipment arrived in Morocco. Pro-Western FLN leaders attempted to remove the Soviet-inspired FLN generals. The pro-Soviet FLN generals promptly supported Ben Bella and formed a Politburo, successfully destroying the pro-Western Algerian leadership.

Also in 1962 Malinovsky was visited by the South Vietnamese rebel leaders in Moscow. One could assume a newly intensified war in South Vietnam. The Siberian Army clique, in this slow piecemeal fashion, sought to undermine the military unity of the West.

In the end, they are attempting to break the alliance of the Western or Atlantic powers as demanded by Soviet military foreign policy. This attempt will, perhaps, succeed without war.

The conclusion reached is that, in recent years and in future years, Soviet policy has been and will be largely determined by the military, heading the power structure within Russia. Through this can be traced the thread of the elite Siberian Army.

With an eye to this army and its leaders, many seemingly unconnected actions of the Soviets in the world can be recognized as linked. This thought helps unwrap the riddle of power in Russia.

SECTION III: / POST-CUBA

THE KGB AND SOVIET POWER POLITICS

The Role of Aleksandr Shelepin

INTRODUCTION

Since the fall of Nikita Khrushchev, on October 13, 1964, many articles, such as one in the *London Observer* of November 30, 1964, have made reference to the revival of the influence of the Soviet Secret Police on Soviet politics. Information in the *Observer* article comes from close to official sources and probably represents the best that U.S. and British intelligence have been able to piece together concerning the events of October 13, 1964, in Moscow. This theory was first brought to light by a team of syndicated columnists, Rowland Evans and Robert Novak, working for the *New York Herald Tribune*. Their theory, linking Nikolai Podgorny, Aleksandr Shelepin, and the KGB, predicted Shelepin's rise to the Presidium. They see the present source of power in Moscow as a revived KGB or Secret Police, suggesting that those leaders of the KGB, both past and present, by virtue of their control over the KGB, have controlled the fortunes of the Soviet Union. They picture the KGB as a worldwide intelligence organization with a domestic spy system radiating from Moscow, capable of taking action and making decisions on its own.

The Major Problem of the Theory

Our intelligence people tend to view their opposites in their own image. Thus, a major fault with the above theory is the probability of overrating or underrating one's opposition based on one's projected feelings. The information and facts gathered in propounding this theory must be examined to determine what is fact; in this vein, the KGB theory should be questioned as to its more basic substance.

Inconsistencies Within the Theory

If one were to have exerted leadership in the Soviet Union, historically, one would also have had to control his source of power directly. Old OGPU, Checka, and NKVD chiefs lasted as powers in Russia only so long as they were in control of the organization. Brezhnev is first secretary of the party and Kosygin is the industry spokesman, but Shelepin is three years removed from his official control of the KGB. One would suspect, then, that the KGB is not his true power base. If history serves correctly, and if the KGB were as powerful as the theory would suggest, then Semichastny (the head of the KGB) would now be a member of the Presidium.

Shelepin is now head of the Party-State Control Commission. This commission has an unknown quantity of power which must be defined. As its name implies, it has the ability to set the rules, and this power separates the rulers from the ruled. No one previously has used the Party-State Commission as a stepping stone to power. Thus, Shelepin's power and true position are in doubt.

According to the *Observer* article, Frol Kozlov is considered an early opponent of Khrushchev. If this were true, then he would have been on the same side as those who plotted against Khrushchev. His quick removal from the Presidium, however, suggests the opposite. Discounting Khrushchev himself, there were ten living members of the Presidium on October 13, 1964.

The article reports that only nine were present at the meeting; one member was missing. Whether it was Kozlov, a friend or enemy of Khrushchev, is not explained.

One questions the veracity of reports that Frol Kozlov had a stroke, Anastas Mikoyan had cancer, and Mikhail Suslov had tuberculosis, particularly if their presence in important decision-making were unwise. Medical illness provides a convenient excuse and avoids embarrassing questions. It would appear that long-term "strain" is an etiological basis for political rather than medical "stroke."

If the KGB is the major power in Russia, then it would seem logical that it would enforce its own rules. Yet, in the Black Sea riots in 1962, army units, instead of KGB, were used. Going further back in time, few KGB troops participated in crushing the 1956 Hungarian uprising.

It is yet to be explained why nine men of an all-important Presidium would elect a man who would eliminate many of them from positions of power. It is also a question why Pyotor Shelest rose to the Presidium at the same time as did Shelepin.

In view of the revival of the Beria-style NKVD (KGB), the organization's objectives and role would have to be clarified. The NKVD's military power was broken by the army in 1953. Beria, as well as other NKVD commanders, was destroyed in 1953, not in 1958-61, as the article reported. Why should Beria be destroyed in 1958, five years after the purge of the Secret Police responsible for the terror of the Stalinist years? The article suggests that the KGB finally purged the NKVD men in 1958. Yet, in 1953, the NKVD had already been broken into a civilian force and a military arm, the latter brought directly under the Ministry of Defense. The civilian branch of the NKVD survived as the KGB. In short, the KGB retained no control whatever over a large portion of the old NKVD. Ivan Serov, defecting from the NKVD to the Soviet Army in 1953, led the military intelligence section of the army and was not purged until 1962. He fell from favor then as a result of his poor handling of information concerning the Cuban crisis. Serov and others were beyond Shelepin's influence and ability to purge. For Shelepin to have ruled the

66

KGB until 1961, while Serov ruled its military equivalent until 1962, suggests that Shelepin never controlled all the sources of power ascribed to him.

Tentative Conclusions

The *Observer* article indicates that intelligence sources learned that Shelepin would rise to the Presidium after Khrushchev had fallen. From the few available facts (that Khrushchev did fall, that he had a confrontation with the Presidium and the Central Committee, and that he was living), Shelepin's rise opened the gates of speculation. After noting that Shelepin had a security and intelligence background, intelligence personnel in the West built a theory in their own image to explain his advancement. For the present there would seem to be enough unanswered questions to shed doubt on the KGB theory; until more facts are available, the theory is relegated to the realm of fantasy.

The Role of Shelepin—A Countertheory

From 1943 to 1952 Shelepin was identified in various positions of leadership in the Komsomol. It is worthwhile here to reconstruct the important role of the Komsomol in Soviet life. It was created before World War II to reinforce the ties between Soviet youth and the regime. While the older population could remember better days, it was the ambitious youth who tied their futures and loyalties to the Red state, who filled the depleted ranks of the Soviet Army with officers and commissars from the Komsomol military schools, who gave civilian support to the defense of Moscow, Leningrad, and Stalingrad. Dmitri Polyanski, a member of the Presidium, traces his political beginnings to his role of Komsomol leader at Stalingrad. Today the Komsomol continues as the early training ground for later Soviet leadership.

The Komsomol maintains the allegiance of youth to the state, regardless of the twists and turns taken by Soviet politics. Because Shelepin is a master at reinterpreting new rules laid down by shifting Presidiums, he has proved invaluable since World War II, accomplishing his propaganda tasks without upsetting the legitimacy of the Soviet government.

Shelepin's later role of interpreting new Presidium rules to the KGB reinforces the theory that he is but a link in a communications chain and not an individual who controls his own source of power. As a member of the Party-State Control Commission, he remained one of the censors and reinterpreters of the changing rules of life in the Soviet Union. If Shelepin is to be considered a source of power, then that power must be defined as the respect of the younger leadership of the Komsomol and his ability to influence the people to follow the party line.

The KGB is not Shelepin's base of operations. Rather, his strength lies in his ability as a manipulator, both of large groups and of man as a political animal. Without the immediate power base of such men as Brezhnev (the army) and Kosygin (the army and the technocrats), however, Shelepin cannot be considered an immediate candidate for succeeding or removing either Brezhnev or Kosygin.

Conclusion

Shelepin's elevation to the Presidium came as a reward for his ability as a master propagandist. His role does not indicate a threat to the present power structure. He will continue to be the interpreter of new Soviet policy for Soviet citizens and for the world. He is neither the ruler nor the ruled, but he is the individual who interprets the rules and conventions of the ruler.

WHY KHRUSHCHEV REMEMBERS

I was first introduced to Kremlinology in the summer of 1962 when, studying Russian history, I speculated that Leonid Brezhnev was the man who would succeed Nikita Khrushchev. Russian history professors at schools in the New York area informed me that this would never be.

My theory was based on the politics of the elite Soviet Army, formed in Siberia in 1920 by Vasily Bleucher. This army's victory over foreign and anti-Soviet forces was aided by Political Commissars Ivan Konev, Konstantin Rokossovsky and Rodion Malinovsky. The Siberian Army played a major role in World War II, both in saving the city of Moscow and in the Battle of Stalingrad. Their final glory of the war was written as Konev's army took Prague, Rokossovsky's army took Warsaw, and Malinovsky's army took Budapest, Bucharest, Belgrade, and Vienna. In 1953, these generals of the Siberian Army, together with the generals who had trained and commanded in European Russia, destroyed the power of the NKVD and promoted Khrushchev, a man with whom they had all worked well at Stalingrad, to first secretary of the Communist Party. I identify this group as left-wing pro-Trotskyite generals.

Khrushchev's falling out with these powerful marshals occurred in 1962, following an attempted power play in Cuba by Khrushchev and dissident army right-wing (pro-Stalinist) generals who wanted to break the strength of the Siberian Army generals. When the power play failed, Khrushchev's days in power were numbered, as had been the days of Zhukov and the antiparty group similarly purged in 1957 after the Hungarian and Polish counterrevolution. It was the supporters of the Siberian Army within the Politburo who were then to succeed Khrushchev. This included Brezhnev, famous for the virgin-lands programs in Siberia, and Kosygin, builder of the Siberian industrial complexes.

The deaths of Rokossovsky and Malinovsky in 1967-68 brought about a great change in the Soviet Union. Ivan Konev, governor general of Czechoslovakia from 1945 to 1951, was now the most powerful Soviet military and political figure. He was thus able to order the Soviet troops into Czechoslovakia even though he was unable to convince many other generals that this act was appropriate. He had to turn to non-Siberian-trained elements—right-wing pro-Stalinist generals of the Soviet Army—for support, as well as to the Soviet Air Force and Soviet Navy. At the same time as he was consolidating his power and position, a great purge was underway. Within a year more than a hundred Soviet generals died of "natural causes" such as old age or accidents. The most important of these generals was Marshal Penkovsky, whose grandnephew had brought tales of the Cuban missile adventure out of the Soviet Union to the West in 1962. After his grandnephew's "treachery" Penkovsky was promoted to head the Siberian Army and later to head the land forces in the Soviet Union. It is possible that the attempted assassination of Brezhnev in May, 1968, may have quickened the demise of those who opposed Konev.

The brilliance of Kosygin's foreign policy from 1964 to 1967 began to pay great dividends, and the Soviet Union was able to extend its domain from building potential nuclear submarine bases in Cuba to a position of dominance in the Mediterranean, the Red Sea, and the Indian Ocean. It pushed ahead its aircraft program as well, building an SST, new fighter planes, and new missiles. The navy and air force received increasing allotments, perhaps for having supported Konev.

Recognizing the power of Konev and the army, the Politburo tried to appoint a civilian head of the Ministry of Defense to succeed Malinovsky. The army balked at this, saying that if Konev's chief of staff during World War II, Marshal Grechko, were not named to the position, then Ivan Konev himself would have to be minister of defense. The Politburo assented, and Grechko, continuing to support the military growth of the Soviet Union, began cutting back the economic advances in the consumer sphere. In this Soviet contest between guns and butter, the guns had won while the consumer economy was forced to suffer.

A split within the Politburo developed as a result of the strivings of the intellectuals against the increased military expenditures. Brezhnev, to continue the policy of heavy industrial growth, sided with Konev. Other members of the Politburo recognized that, to continue this military expansion, Stalinist methods of repression against dissident groups had been reintroduced. Khrushchev's memoirs, then, were a key to what was happening and should be interpreted as a cry for help by the dissident elements within the Politburo and the army.

The messages of Khrushchev's memoirs are clear: the Stalinist era had returned; the generals in power were cracking down on dissidence. Continued American acceptance of détente would allow Soviet military expansion; the dissident, anti-Stalinist group needed world support to stop the return of the Stalinist repression. Those in the Soviet Union interested in domestic expansion would be helped by an unwavering, hard-line American position. Thus, opening borders, a favorable outcome at the SALT talks, a winding down of the Vietnam War, and peace in the Middle East would help those opposed to the return of the Stalinists with their paranoid ideas.

One has the feeling that when Khrushchev talks about Robert Kennedy's discussions of the possible military overthrow of John Kennedy during the Cuban Missile Crisis he is implying that the right-wing Russian military could do this to those in the Politburo who oppose the hard-line policies. Khrushchev refers to the last Stalinist purge, against the Jewish doctors at Leningrad, in which Stalin was reputedly aiming at these high-ranking members of the Soviet government, one of them Kosygin. The return eighteen years later of the Jewish trials in Leningrad indicates the return of a putsch in the Soviet Union against high ranking officials such as Kosygin, which the publication of the memoirs could possibly stop.

That Khrushchev's memoirs were allowed to leave the country is further indication that some Politburo members felt the pressure of the return of Stalinist ideas. Joseph Alsop suggested that Aleksandr Shelepin was Mr. X, the man in the Politburo responsible for the release of the memoirs. I would suggest that Mr. X was Aleksei Kosygin and his left-wing army supporters. At the time that Khrushchev was ill and hospitalized, Kosygin was also hospitalized for three months, a long enough time for Mr. X to edit and rewrite those parts of the memoirs printed in *Life* magazine, to warn the West, as the "Penkovsky Papers" once did, that Western help could sway the Politburo to a more pacific tact.

In my opinion there are hard-line elements within the Soviet government who are amenable to the carrot-and-stick approach. By denouncing any efforts within the Soviet Union to tighten controls against its people and by attempting to reach accord with the Soviet Politburo on the major political issues of our time, the hardliners would easily retreat. Perhaps Khrushchev or the real Mr. X who wrote the book is really saying *never again* to the return of the Stalinists.

PART II / THE AMERICAN FALL

INTRODUCTION

I suspect that the American Fall reflects what psychiatrists would call a post-Vietnam syndrome, which does not occur until 18 to 24 months after leaving the army. The initial optimism of the Kennedy era is reflected in the article "American Medicine as a Military-Political Weapon" (1966). The questioning of our involvement in Vietnam led to the article on "American National Interest Defined." Of all the articles, this one reflected almost seven years of research, for it was the American scene which was the most difficult to understand. The challenge was to synopsize two hundred years into a continuity that was comprehensible. Unfortunately, American foreign policy, which is hinged on a 1940 idealism, is rushing toward bankruptcy without a coherent new domestic or foreign policy arising.

The last concept introduced in this part is the elite army unit, which plays a major role in history. It is discussed here so the reader may inquire as to whether the elite army unit does have a place on the American scene.

DRAMATIS PERSONAE

The Players (in some order of importance)

Benjamin Harrison, signer of Declaration of Independence (1726-1791)

James Wilson, Supreme Court Justice (1742-1798)

Daniel Morgan, Revolutionary War General (1736-1802)

William Henry Harrison, President of the United States (1773-1841)

Benjamin Harrison, President of the United States (1833-1901)

John Tyler, President of the United States (1790-1862)

George Henry Thomas, Union General (1816-1870)

James Harrison Wilson, Union General (1837-1925)

Elihu Root, Statesman (1845-1937)

Arthur MacArthur, Lieutenant General of the Army (1845-1912)

Douglas MacArthur, General of the Army (1880-1964)

John Foster, Secretary of State (1836-1917)

John Foster Dulles, Secretary of State (1888-1959)

Robert Lansing, Secretary of State (1864-1928)

Felix Frankfurter, Supreme Court Justice (1882-1965)

Leonard Wood, first Chief of Staff of the Army (1860-1927)

Henry Lewis Stimson, Secretary of War (1867-1950)

Harvey Bundy, Assistant Secretary of War (1888-1963)

McGeorge Bundy, President, Ford Foundation (1919-   )

William Bundy, Editor, Foreign Affairs Quarterly (1917-   )

Dean Acheson, Secretary of State (1893-1971)

Henry Kissinger, Secretary of State (1923-   )

KEY ACTS

SECTION I / AMERICAN MEDICINE AS A MILITARY-POLITICAL WEAPON

Experience has shown that medicine has been one of the most consistently successful instruments for stabilizing insurgencies. Major General Leonard Wood and General of the Army Douglas MacArthur specifically employed American medicine to gain an effective initial access to alien cultures; their utilization of medicine immediately and positively affected the lives of entire populations. Inherent in American medicine and rooted in Western culture are democratic and humanistic value systems which Wood and MacArthur introduced into other societies through military medical practice.

American medicine is still being successfully utilized this way, as Special Forces medical aides experience the ease of access and acceptance of Western man and his medicine into alien cultures. Color slides reveal the Green Beret medic with a portable dispensary on his medical rounds, protected by Mao tribesmen in Laos and by Montagnard tribesmen in South Vietnam. Local tribesmen bring the Special Forces medic from village to village, introducing him to people viewing Americans for the first time.

United States involvement in the Caribbean as well as in the Pacific shows that successful stability operations in cross-cultural environments occur when commanders demonstrate a broad awareness of the need for community medical and public health measures. Particular success in civil administration has marked the path of Leonard Wood and of individuals who served under Wood, such as Major General Frank McCoy and Douglas MacArthur. Gains achieved in Cuba, in the Philippines, and in Japan under the administration of these men are among the finest accomplishments of America's role in nation-building. Their achievements followed from the knowledge and use of broad civic-action programs, with medicine as the cornerstone.

Wood's credentials in counterinsurgency are the finest of any twentieth-century general; yet Wood and his use of medicine in military-political wars have been forgotten by most people. Wood first participated in a small phase of the military campaign which resulted in the pacification of the Chiricua Apaches and the capture of Geronimo. Rebel Apaches in the southwestern deserts of the United States and in northern Mexico were the guerrillas who led Wood's expedition on a 1,500-mile pursuit, and Wood's actions were rewarded by a Medal of Honor in 1886. Later recognition of Wood's military capacities came when he commanded regulars and Rough Riders in action near Santiago de Cuba in the Spanish-American War. Wood's commission was as a colonel of volunteers in Cuba. In the Regular Army, Wood was a captain in the Medical Corps; later he became the only Medical Corps officer to rise to chief of staff of the United States Army (1911–13).

Wood's initial experience in the field of civic action and civil administration occurred in Santiago de Cuba, after the Spanish-American War ended. He began with a massive cleanup of the carnage of battle and of the garbage left by years of an inefficient Spanish collection system. Efforts to improve sanitation were followed by the re-creation of a potable water supply in the city, the first in twenty years. A system of local civil government instituted by Wood provided a sounding-board by which Cubans expressed interest in civic improvements; in 1902 these locally created civil governments became the first independent governments in Cuban history.

In addition, Wood brought the Cuban Negro into the mainstream of Cuban life, after he sensed elements of discord or prejudice between the older Spanish-Cuban elite and the Negro. As governor-general of all Cuba (1900), Wood increased the educational budget, strengthened the judiciary to maintain civil rights, and slowly integrated the diverse segments of the population.

Another problem which Wood faced was that of the health hazards in Cuba, which were excessive for American soldiers. A Walter Reed medical investigatory team was dispatched to Cuba; without Wood's strong backing, Reed's victory in isolating the yellow fever vector would not have occurred. A by-product of Wood's interest in the health of the American soldier was demonstrated by the removal of Americans from the disease-ridden lowland cities to the highlands, which also contributed to the lessening of tension between Cubans and U.S. forces.

Wood's success in Cuba was followed by his being appointed to administer the provinces of the Moros in the Philippines. American administrators in the Philippines had faced a constant insurrection. The appointment of Wood in 1902 to pacify the last insurgents, the Moros, was made in recognition of his abilities, which had blunted any possible Cuban national insurrection against the brief American rule in Cuba. Wood's mission in the Philippines was to assure the Moslems of their future role in a Catholic land. Major successes in pacification followed Wood's utilization of civic-action projects throughout the Moslem islands.

Sanitation and public health measures were introduced. Thomasites, American teachers brought over on the troopship *Thomas* from the U.S., were utilized by Wood to attack illiteracy. Many soldiers were also used as teachers in projects that presaged efforts of the Special Forces and the Peace Corps. Effective civic policy resulted in steadily increasing local responsibilities within the framework of the military government. Wood's sensitivity to varying local conditions brought about a smooth transition for many ethnic groups from community isolation to provincial interaction. Wood had learned to incorporate diverse groups of people, at different stages of development, into the blueprint of nation-building in his early tours in Cuba and the Philippines.

After a fourteen-year absence, Wood returned to the Philippines in 1921 only to find serious defects in the process of Filipino nation-building. A major setback in the program was the achievement of primacy of one ethnic group in the national government, which had taken place under the previous governor-general. Ethnic minorities were receiving little representation in Manila, while the Filipino-Spanish ruling elite were demanding increasingly greater autonomy. Further autonomy would have allowed the elite to perpetuate their interests to the detriment of the ethnic minorities.

Wood now saw his task as that of allowing all segments of the population to develop political and economic responsibility; he refused to allow the ruling elite to govern the country without considering the aspirations and needs of all segments of the population. Meanwhile, representatives of the Filipino elite had established a headquarters in Washington and were attempting to spread detrimental propaganda about Wood. As a result, an investigating committee was formed, sent to the Philippines, and allowed to tour the provinces. The committee's findings, reached by talking with members of all ethnic groups, held only praise for Wood's efforts in nation-building.

Later in 1926 Wood replaced Filipinos responsible for continued mismanagement in the government with American staff advisors who promoted effective central government for all Filipinos. Wood died in 1927, before he could see the success of his policies as governor-general of the Philippines; however, the continued loyalty of the Filipino minority groups during World War II, represented by Ramon Magsaysay and other World War II guerrilla leaders, attests to the wealth of good feeling which the United States accrued through Wood's efforts in the Philippines.

Frank McCoy, an infantry officer aide to Wood in Cuba and in the Philippines, was responsible for the administration of many of Wood's public health measures and humane policies, first on a local and then on a worldwide scale. Even more important was McCoy's "behind-the-scenes" role of emphasizing the ethical values of American institutions. McCoy was a member of the Nicaragua Commission that brought peace to a troubled Nicaragua in 1927.

McCoy's interest in Latin America sowed the seeds of the Good Neighbor Policy. He rose to be president of the Council on Foreign Relations (1938-45). From this position he gently prodded the hemisphere's conscience and struggled to bring the Good Neighbor Policy to the world. Many achievements of the Council on Foreign Relations may be attributed to McCoy's interest in furthering the relationship between Americans and various alien ethnic groups of the world. The founding of the United Nations, with its representative branches in education (UNESCO), Labor (ILO), and Medicine (WHO), was in part due to the specific interest of Frank McCoy and the Council on Foreign Relations.

Douglas MacArthur, who acted as aide to Wood in Washington (1911) and in the Philippines (1922), later amply demonstrated in Japan the powerful effects of the use of American medicine in producing good will toward American aims. MacArthur's medical program literally reached every Japanese citizen after World War II. In 1946 a medical team under Brigadier General Crawford F. Sams developed a program in which 80,000,000 Japanese were vaccinated against smallpox. Reemphasizing America's interest in the health and welfare of the population, a like number of Japanese were revaccinated in 1949. Without regard to race, religion, or culture, the scourge of smallpox was removed from Japan. In addition, one out of every two Japanese citizens was dusted with DDT; there was an 86 percent decrease in diphtheria rates; 36,000,000 Japanese were immunized against tuberculosis with BCG vaccines; and 34,000,000 persons were immunized against cholera. As a result of this massive program, tuberculosis decreased in incidence, cholera was eliminated entirely from Japan after December, 1946, and dysentery, typhoid, and paratyphoid almost disappeared in Japan. The medical program depended on the establishment of 800 health centers, each staffed by 100 men and women. Additionally, 100,000 six-man teams worked out of these centers, going from street to street checking the water supply, demonstrating sanitation methods, and teaching preventive medicine. MacArthur's program under Crawford Sams made Japan a twentieth-century nation in the field of public health.

MacArthur's first directive to the Japanese as supreme commander was a bill of rights issued on October 4, 1945, removing all "restrictions on political, civil, and religious liberties on the ground of race, nationality, creed, or public opinion." The Japanese themselves administered the Civil Liberties Bureau, which enforced the new "law of the land." MacArthur deflated the importance of the elite Shinto class, and he allowed complete freedom of worship. Catholic, Protestant and Buddhist advisors were placed in a religious advisory section of Supreme Headquarters. MacArthur also decentralized the educational system; he allowed the local authorities to elect their own school boards, to choose their own textbooks, and to appoint their own school superintendents. In 1947, a school education law guaranteed equal elementary school educational opportunity. Two other major MacArthur accomplishments were in the fields of labor legislation and land reform. Labor unions were created and almost 5,000,000 acres of Japanese land were redistributed.

MacArthur's accomplishments allowed the broadest fulfillment of Wood's visions. The pacification of Japan, her rise to postwar heights, and her democratic processes are among the best examples of American foreign policy in action. One wonders why MacArthur and Wood have outshone other American administrators in their sensitivity vis-à-vis the problems of ethnic minorities. Perhaps their unique experience on the Indian frontier made them more sensitive to the plight of minorities. As the future chiefs-of-staff awaited later years of command and glory, they viewed the frustrations and sensed the feelings of the children of the Sioux, the Apaches, and other Indian nations. Frontier years revealed firsthand the injustices which the nonunderstanding visited upon the weak. Perhaps Wood as a young soldier and MacArthur as a child on the frontier carried their Indian experiences as a burden to be relieved; perhaps older Indian fighters (Major General Nelson A. Miles and Lieutenant General Arthur MacArthur) who had grown to respect their foes influenced the young Wood and MacArthur.

One must also wonder if the enlightened field- and company-grade military officers of the present will understand the vast differences between ethnic groups and will recognize that medicine has a major role in filling these cross-cultural gaps. Perhaps the young officer in training can be made sensitive to the plight of the ethnically underprivileged through exposure to such groups as the American Indian, the Alaskan Eskimo, the backwoodsman of Appalachia, and the Negro of many areas of America. The insights gained from the underprivileged and ethnically isolated, and the rediscovery of the ethical values of the professed Good Neighbor creed, might produce enlightened officers who can effectively cope with the major political-military problems of wars of national liberation. In addition, future education of military civic-action personnel might include the relearning of successful civil-affairs lessons as taught by Wood and MacArthur.

Today, young medical officers have questioned whether American medical personnel will be accepted in the Orient in quest of a so-far elusive victory in Vietnam. Historically, Western medicine has been the key to the Oriental home and has unlocked a store of goodwill for Western man entering an Eastern world. After the Boxer Rebellion in China (1900), Yale, Harvard and Pennsylvania universities established medical facilities in urban environments to teach Chinese students. Medical schools under American sponsorship in Shanghai and Peking allowed the further ease of flow of Western humanistic and scientific ideas to China. For nearly a century American medical missionaries added to the growing practice of public health in Asia. In addition, American foundations (e.g., the Rockefeller Foundation) exported and established medical research facilities which were recognized worldwide. The good feeling engendered by medical schools, medical missionaries and medical research facilities allows the Western physician continued acceptance into Eastern cultures.

The Sino-Japanese War (1931-45) and the post-World War II Chinese Civil War brought an end to American involvement in Chinese medicine. Perhaps the failure of American political-military missions to stabilize China between 1942 and 1949 could be based partially on the inability during World War II to utilize medicine as an opening gambit in approaching turmoil-ridden China. Chiang Kai-shek specifically pleaded with American military personnel to understand an Oriental psychology which was susceptible to the approach of Western medicine. A sidelight to the story of the understanding of medicine in Oriental psychology occurred when Chiang originally went to the Soviet Union to seek aid for the Sun Yat-sen revolution in 1923.

Chiang was rewarded with a political-military mission under a Russian leader whose pseudonym was of a Roman physician, Galen. The fact that Wood, the well-known American physician, was only a few hundred miles away, as governor-general of the Philippines, may have influenced the Russian leader in his choice of a pseudonym to exploit the store of good feeling the Chinese had for the image of the Western physician.

To close the vast cultural gaps between ethnic groups, enlightened military officers used American medicine to heal the sick, American physicians and medics to train thousands of public health workers, and the faculties of major American universities to organize medical schools. In the 1960s, greater medical and public health instruments were available than in previous times; however, significant gulfs of minority and cultural (religious and ethnic) discrimination which elude solution are still found in Vietnam and around the world. Ten years of independence have not brought the Vietnamese ethnic minorities the first-class citizenship that Wood, McCoy, and MacArthur found most important in nation-building.

In the past there has been a lack of appreciation and use of the political weapons of medicine, sanitation and education in the interest of minority groups. Today a growing awareness of the importance of medicine as an instrument of national policy led to the commitment of public health teams to Vietnam. Experience would seem to indicate that the health team is readily accepted by various minority groups, when the effort serves as an indication to the people that *their own government* is concerned with their welfare.

Once accepted, such teams may plan for the implementation of hospital-educational complexes which will contribute to the upgrading of the health and educational standards of specific minority groups. The training of medical paraprofessional personnel—

medics, nurses, laboratory technicians, and teachers—drawn from the people of a national minority can lead to further acceptance of Western ideas and ideals. Subsequently, the minority group may be led to a wish to provide its own military contribution to the central government as a response to a feeling of conciliation and concern on the part of the government, demonstrated through introduction of modern medicine and education.

While previous American policy has not been entirely clear in past interactions with various ethnic minority groups in Vietnam, future American policy might well express itself in the health, education, and welfare of all Vietnamese minorities and ethnic groups. Such an effort might be directed both toward the minorities and toward the central government, in an effort to create and maintain a bond of mutual trust between divergent cultures, through medicine. It is not inconceivable that such a policy would lead to a stabilization of cross-cultural relationships, and might contribute in some way to a solution to the South Vietnamese insurgency.

SECTION II / AMERICAN NATIONAL INTEREST DEFINED

Individuals find it fruitless to try to learn why we were in Vietnam; they were merely told in vague terms that it was in "the American national interest." In refining the question, perhaps we can come to better answers as to our involvement in the world. The question we must ask is: Who has defined American national interest? By listing the individuals who have given this definition continuity for about two hundred years, we can come to the principles of their policy which have led us to our present role in the world.

The original definition of American national interest arose from the policymaking capabilities of two committees of the Continental Congress in 1775. The first was the Board of War, and the second was the Committee on Secret Correspondence, which dealt with foreign affairs. America, an unrecognized country, had its foreign affairs carried on unofficially and secretly. Benjamin Harrison was a member of both committees and; for the first years of emerging America, he was instrumental in setting policy goals for the country.

Benjamin Harrison was a fifth-generation Virginia Harrison, a scion of one of the wealthiest colonial families, able to trace his family tree to kings of England. A member of the Virginia House of Burgesses, he was friendly with all the other powerful Virginians who came to play a role in the Revolution. His interests lay in his tidewater plantation as well as in western land speculation, an interest he shared with George Washington, a fellow plantation owner and surveyor of western lands.

British foreign policy and statutes drawn up after the French and Indian Wars (1756–1763) had restricted American colonial interests in land beyond the Appalachians. But Virginia planters and other colonial peoples looked westward for the future economic expansion of the country. The clash of foreign-policy interests between crown and colonies was one of the cornerstones of the Revolution.

Benjamin Harrison, acting in his capacity as chairman of the two major policy-making committees, formulated two policies of national interest that remain with us today: first, that our destiny lay in the expansion of the country across the Appalachians into the West and beyond, and second, that America should fight any war as far as possible from domestic shores.

Although the colonials professed concern for the freedom of the Thirteen Colonies, America's first major military expedition occurred in Canada. First a thousand and then ten thousand men traveled northward to Canada to divert limited British resources. Harrison's plan was finally delineated during the conquest of Boston in 1775 with the concurrence of Washington, Benedict Arnold, and a successful Virginia Indian fighter named Daniel Morgan. Before independence, Harrison's Virginia was already clearing its western borders of Indians and had thus created an effective band of fighters. Arnold and Morgan's column was sent up the Kennebec River in Maine to Quebec City. A second New York column, under General Richard Montgomery, seized Montreal. Then both columns met at Quebec City and took the lower undefended city on Christmas, 1775. Minutes separated the colonials from victory within the entire city and the conquest of Canada. Had Canada been taken, the British, to regain possession of the St. Lawrence Valley, would have been forced to divert the very limited number of men they could transport to the colonies by sea. British hegemony over the St. Lawrence allowed them the potential to strike down through New York, cutting the colonies in two. In 1776, 10,000 Americans were sent into upper New

York State to try to wrest control of Canada. Again, the American effort was thwarted. This diversion did allow Benjamin Harrison and the other founding fathers to publish the Declaration of Independence in a seaport city far from the battlefields, without interference.

These were not our last expeditions into Canada. "Continental union" was the rubric by which dreams of American hegemony over North America were expressed, even into the twentieth century. Today we still read about Canada being incorporated into the United States as additional states.

In the area of foreign affairs Harrison had linked American foreign policy to that of Spain, France and Holland. A successful battle by the Americans would bring further arms, money, and a fleet. Showing his ability to select the finest military commanders, Harrison again placed Daniel Morgan in New York State. At the Battle of Freeman's Farm, Morgan was instrumental in winning the decisive victory at Saratoga. It was this victory in the American Revolution which ushered in a worldwide war in which Britain stood alone.

Harrison returned to Virginia from Philadelphia to continue to execute the policies he felt were in the American national interest but which had been frustrated by a divided Continental Congress that could not act. As Speaker of the House of Burgesses, Harrison raised a 200-man expedition under the leadership of George Rogers Clark to conquer the Midwest for the United States. Clark and his men successfully fought their way to Detroit in the most meaningful American adventure beyond the Thirteen Colonies. In 1779, Massachusetts also tried a separate $7-million military expedition to Nova Scotia, which failed and bankrupted the state.

The importance of Harrison as the definer of national interest should not be underrated. When Benedict Arnold abandoned the American Revolution, he was given a British expedition to break the back of American power. Arnold chose to raid tidewater Virginia, where he burned the Harrison estate and found Harrison's correspondence with Washington. With more men, Arnold could have seized Harrison, who continued directing from afar the interests of newborn America.

Virginian interest in western lands was shared by Pennsylvanians. On the 1775 Board of War was James Wilson, a Pennsylvanian who was to be a future Supreme Court member. His interests also lay in western land speculation. According to the historian Charles Beard, about 25 percent of the men who led in the founding of the republic had western land interests. Western land speculation was to be a future source of wealth for those who held land rights, and especially for those who held the choice lands along the rivers as these could be sold to the burgeoning American population. Success in opening up the western regions came slowly. The lack of a strong central power during the Articles of Confederacy and the first Washington years forced many speculators into bankruptcy. James Wilson was cornered by his creditors in 1792, and in succession he resigned from the Supreme Court and committed suicide.

Western land speculation was hindered by the British, the Indians, the lack of an army, and the lack of a strong central power. Washington, after consolidating federal power, founded the first peacetime army to break the Indian threat. The American Legion under Anthony Wayne destroyed the Indian power in western New York State. Benjamin Harrison's third son, William Henry Harrison, in the expansionist tradition of his father, was an ensign in this campaign. As a young man and protégé of Washington, he quickly gained positions as territorial representative and territorial governor of the Northwest Territories. He was governor of Ohio, Indiana, and Illinois, and when the Louisiana Purchase was made in 1803, it was William Henry Harrison who ruled everything north of modern Louisiana. He married Anne Cleves Symmes, whose father manipulated and sold downtown Cincinnati and other western lands. Harrison himself is not implicated in any financial speculations; rather, he is the prototype military-political figure as consul of empire. Harrison was involved in constant treaty-making with the Indians, securing land for further colonization, and driving the Indians beyond the Mississippi. The fact that there was only one major battle (Tippecanoe) during the twenty years of Harrison's service as a consul of empire shows the success of his policies.

William Henry Harrison was able to cross party lines. Appointed by Federalists like John Adams, he was continued in power by Thomas Jefferson. Jefferson supported further western expansion and launched the Lewis and Clark Expedition to the Pacific. William was George Rogers Clark's brother. Thus, America's race to Mars and beyond progressed.

William Henry Harrison continued in the family tradition of expansion by invading Canada during the War of 1812. Of all the generals who invaded Canada he was the most successful. After the naval victory of Oliver Hazard Perry in Lake Erie, Harrison pushed deep into Canada, only to be turned back by logistics difficulties and the weather. One notes that Oliver's brother, Commodore Matthew Perry, opened Japan to American commerce and influence in 1853-54.

Harrison continued to represent the Midwest and to maintain his connections to Virginia. In an era of territorial compromises and admission of new states to the Union, Harrison played an important role in raising his voice above sectional interests in order to speak for national interests. When Jacksonian democracy brought further sectional strife to the country, Harrison became a source of unifying influence. From 1836 to 1840 he stifled sectionalism and supported national institutions. On his own, William Henry Harrison continued the dream of expansion. On his mind were both the entrance into the Union of the new Republic of Texas and America's expansion into these western territories then under Mexican and Texan authorities. Harrison's own son, as a spy, reported faithfully to his father the nature of the new Mexican lands to be opened to American expansion.

After fifty years of service to America, William Henry Harrison became President in 1840. His running mate was John Tyler, whose father had been a very close friend, ally and neighbor of Benjamin Harrison in the days of the Virginia Burgesses. "Tippecanoe and Tyler too" reflected a sectional and familial relationship that spanned generations. Harrison's death within a month of taking office did not end the Harrison interests in expansion. John Tyler was also to try to annex Texas; his final act as President was to achieve a 36-23 vote for annexation, a vote which narrowly failed to win the necessary two-thirds majority.

James Polk, Tyler's successor, brought Texas into the Union on a congressional resolution which did not require a two-thirds majority. The concept of Manifest Destiny, usually attributed to Polk and the Mexican War era, had begun in the minds of the Harrisons and was further developed by Tyler and Polk.

Although Tyler had been frustrated by the Texas issue, he had achieved a *modus operandi* with the English. A Maine boundary settlement in 1842 was quickly followed by an amicable Oregon settlement. Tyler already saw that in twenty years America would be a leading, if not the leading, world power. The security of America's borders was paramount, and the emerging English friendship was also to be counted on. The Harrisons were Anglophiles in a Whig tradition. Continued English friendship allowed American commerce to sail unhindered in the Atlantic and Pacific oceans, protected by English maritime might. Meanwhile, America grew domestically, unbothered for the next twenty years, until it was ready to take a leading role in the world scene.

The goal of the preservation of the Union above sectional interests remained important to the Harrisons and the Tylers. Bringing Texas into the Union would balance slave and free states. The definers of national interest flirted briefly with the idea of bringing Mexico into the Union as a slave state, but when emissaries to Mexico reported that she had previously freed her slaves, the idea was dropped, and it was Mexico's attitude toward slavery which saved her from becoming part of the United States. Among southerners Tyler was unique in his desire for Union. In 1861, as a southern peace commissioner, he attempted to maintain, rather than separate, the Union.

In presenting a continuous picture of the select group of men who determined American national interests, it is the Civil War period which represented the most difficult gap to fill. Nevertheless, the continuity was there. During the war the Tyler interests were represented in the North by a Virginian who later became Tyler's brother-in-law, Major General George Henry Thomas. He was the finest Union general of the war. Thomas participated in the largest area of fighting, creating the best fighting units in the war, the Fourteenth Corps and the Army of the Cumberland. It was the Army of the Cumberland which fought in Kentucky, Tennessee, Alabama, and Georgia, and it was the Fourteenth Corps which captured Atlanta and then, under William T. Sherman, marched to the sea. At one point Thomas's chief of staff was General James Garfield, his political commissar was General Andrew Johnson, and a leading general was Benjamin Harrison, the future President. Founders of other future political dynasties, such as the Coxes in Ohio and Palmers in Illinois, were also among Thomas's men.

The Harrison interests had been maintained in Washington by William Henry Harrison's son John. When John Harrison retired from Washington, it was his son Benjamin, the future general and President, who was groomed for leadership. The man most instrumental in maintaining and developing the Harrison tradition was a relative named James Harrison Wilson, named after two original members of the Board of War. From 1861 to 1865 Wilson appeared at most of the major battles of the Civil War. At first he relayed information to the Department of War as to the successes and failures of various Union generals. In time, Wilson, a West Pointer and a good engineer, became a great general in his own right.

He took part in the successful Port Royal-Burnside Expedition which, as the first amphibious assault on southern coasts, produced a base from which the growing Union blockade of southern shores could begin. Wilson then became a member of Grant's staff and was continually helpful to Grant, particularly as an engineer at Vicksburg. Wilson's role on Grant's staff allowed Lincoln to feel more secure with Grant. Grant in turn appointed Wilson inspector general and later commandant of the Cavalry Bureau. The Cavalry Bureau created the Cavalry Corps of Philip Sheridan, who had previously fought beside George Henry Thomas.

One of Thomas's difficulties as a general was the lack of cavalry in the West. With a well trained infantry Thomas had won the first Union victories of the Civil War, and by 1863 his forces had opened the gateway to the South at Missionary Ridge near Chattanooga, Tennessee. One of Thomas's young officer heroes at Missionary Rudge was a Wisconsin colonel, Arthur MacArthur, the father of Douglas MacArthur. In order to continue southward, Thomas needed a cavalry which could match the Confederate cavalry. Wilson assumed command of this western cavalry of 80,000 men. By Christmas, 1864, Wilson and Thomas had won the most outstanding Union military triumph of the war at Nashville. Thirty-two thousand Confederate soldiers were eliminated from the war. Wilson's unit of cavalry, armed with Spencer repeating rifles, swept to the rear of Hood's Confederate force, creating a modern Cannae. By 1865, independent commands of Wilson's cavalry were forty miles from Appomattox in Virginia, had captured Jefferson Davis in Georgia, and had crushed Nathan Bedford Forrest in Selma, Alabama. Wilson's leading cavalry commander was Emory Upton, the finest regimental commander of any unit, whether cavalry, infantry, or artillery, during the Civil War.

The Harrison-Tyler interests in standing for union had been well represented by Thomas and Wilson during the Civil War. After the war it was Thomas and later Grant who became the leading Harrison candidates to succeed Andrew Johnson, who had fallen from favor with the Harrison forces during and after the war. Thomas refused any interest in the Presidency in 1868 and died a year later. Wilson, after initial frustrations with occupational duties, retired from the army, ostensibly to build railroads. Behind the scenes he maintained his interest in both national and international politics. When the Whiskey Scandal threatened to destroy the image of the Grant administration, Wilson suggested that his brother Telford Wilson handle the situation and salvage Grant's reputation. In the foreign-policy arena, Grant, Sherman and other Harrison allies recognized the need for creating a more coherent picture of America's future foreign-policy involvements in the world. Both Wilson and Upton were dispatched around the world to provide directions for the future army and foreign policy. Emory Upton wrote *The Military Policy of the United States*, in which he described the army of the future. His basic concept was to fight foreign wars with an expandable army supported by a buildup of American seapower.

James Garfield read Upton's book and, partially as a result of the book, during Garfield's Presidency the navy was revived after a fifteen-year period of inactivity. Initially these naval plans were embroiled in a controversy remarkably similar to the more modern ABM controversy. Garfield's momentary answer was limiting the battle fleet to coastal-going battleships for defending our shores. By 1889 the concept had shifted so that oceangoing battleships were built to take the war to foreign shores if war were to come. The President who in 1889 had readied the fleet that was to fight in Cuba and the Philippines was Benjamin Harrison.

The Harrison tradition was thus imparted to those who carried it forward to the present time. Under Harrison, foreign policy advisors such as John Foster, William Howard Taft, Theodore Roosevelt, Henry Cabot Lodge, and Alfred Thayer Mahan were first exposed to the Harrison concept of national interest. James Harrison Wilson returned from China and Japan, telling of future markets necessary to the continuance of American economic expansion. Wilson was also to talk of the need for America to control Cuba.

Alfred Thayer Mahan spoke of a great power's need for naval stations; Benjamin Harrison responded with the involvement of the United States in Samoa and Hawaii. Harrison created the modern navy; McKinley and Theodore Roosevelt were to use it. The growing battle fleet stood off Cuba and the Philippines. The *Maine* was sunk, and the War of 1898 followed. Second in command of the Puerto Rican expedition was James Harrison Wilson. Puerto Rico was won almost without firing a shot. It was Wilson who formulated the policies which encouraged Puerto Rico to remain a possession of the United States. After ·his military-political conquest of Puerto Rico, Wilson went to Cuba where he competed with Leonard Wood, a protégé of Roosevelt and McKinley, for the position of governor-general of the island. Wilson lost, but the policies he enunciated in Puerto Rico were the policies which Wood instituted.

During the time of the Harrison administration, further ties to New York law firms were cemented through Whitelaw Reid. Another New Yorker, Elihu Root, became Secretary of War in

1899. A lawyer rather than a military man, Root was brought in specifically to administer plans to pacify and to consolidate the United States interests in Puerto Rico, Cuba and the Philippines. Wilson's correspondence with Root was to become the framework for American foreign-policy involvement in overseas territories in this century. Wilson stressed civic-action projects and, where this was done quickly, as in Cuba and Puerto Rico, counterinsurgency activity did not begin. Where Wilson had not gone, such as the Philippines, the situation exploded. Arthur MacArthur was to pacify the northern provinces and Leonard Wood was to pacify the southern provinces. Governor-generalship of the islands was later given to William Howard Taft, Leonard Wood, and a son of Theodore Roosevelt. Other naval bases acquired were Subic Bay in the Philippines and Guantanamo Bay in Cuba.

At the same time (1900) another decision faced the coterie of people who were determining American foreign policy: how to respond to the Boxer Rebellion. In China, a railroad which had been proposed by James Harrison Wilson and built by Herbert Hoover was under siege. Hoover was trapped at Tsien-tsien and he acted as civil commander of the besieged town. Wilson was second in command of the successful American relief troops in China. Because he had firsthand knowledge of the Chinese situation from his previous travels, he influenced the policy of the open door to Chinese markets.

In 1903 Wilson and Root again corresponded on the issue of a permanent army. Wilson sent Root Emory Upton's *The Military Policy of the United States*. It was Upton's theory that the National Guard divisions of the various states should be part of an expandable army prepared for service on foreign shores. The Army Reorganization Act of 1903 thus followed, and the European wars in which Upton had predicted American involvement could now be met by American troops. Root later became Secretary of State and was succeeded by William Howard Taft. Another New Yorker, Henry L. Stimson, a Theodore Roosevelt protégé, became Secretary of War in 1911. Stimson, a former federal district attorney, brought in Felix Frankfurter as his right-hand man. In World War I Frankfurter served as a leading figure on the War Mobilization Board as well as in the economic life of the country while at war. During World War I a Roosevelt cousin, Franklin Delano Roosevelt, became assistant Secretary of the Navy. Before the war Stimson introduced the general staff system into the army and appointed Leonard Wood as the first chief of staff.

The election of 1912 split the Republican party asunder. Woodrow Wilson's victory brought about a temporary eclipse of the Harrison tradition. Wilson looked at Wood, Roosevelt, and Taft as potential presidential candidates in 1916. Instead, as private citizens, the Harrison heirs laid the foundations for America's entry into World War I. Wood started the Plattsburgh camps, which developed the American Army Officer Corps for World War I. Roosevelt thundered throughout the country, urging preparedness, and in the end the United States went to war. Into Wilson's cabinet came Robert Lansing, the son-in-law of John Foster. John Foster had continued his activity in foreign affairs and in 1903 had attended the Hague Peace Conference with his grandson, John Foster Dulles. Later, at Versailles in 1919, Robert Lansing named his nephew, John Foster Dulles, chief secretary of the American delegation. They came to Versailles on the strength of the victory of the armies created by Emory Upton, James Harrison Wilson, Elihu Root, and Leonard Wood. In 1920 Leonard Wood was the leading Harrison candidate for the Presidency, but he lost to Harding at the Republican national convention.

The era of the 1920s has been noted for its isolationist policies. The continuity in foreign policy was maintained by New York's Wall Street law firms. While Washington basked in the great economic boom of the 1920s, the great Wall Street firms negotiated the flow of over seven billion dollars of private American capital into foreign bonds. The private law firms, the preserves of the Stimsons and the Dulleses (managing partner and partner, Sullivan and Cromwell) reached the zenith of their influence during the 1920s. Herbert Hoover, as Secretary of Commerce for eight years, attempted to guide the American expansion. Occasionally the New York lawyers would be called into government service to negotiate peaceful settlements of foreign disputes. In 1927 Stimson was dispatched to Nicaragua to bring order out of chaos in revolution. Aiding Stimson at this time was Frank McCoy, an aide-de-camp to Leonard Wood in Cuba and a Wood protégé as a military-political figure. In time Frank McCoy was to become the president of the Council of Foreign Affairs, serving from 1939 to 1945. Under McCoy's tutelage the Council became a cornerstone in maintaining the Harrison tradition in our overseas policy. In Nicaragua, Stimson and McCoy were to speak of the new American foreign-policy directions in Latin America which came to be called the Good Neighbor Policy.

In 1928 Herbert Hoover became President and Henry Stimson became Secretary of State. For undersecretary, Stimson chose Harvey Bundy. In 1931, the Japanese attacked Manchuria. Stimson pleaded with his Quaker President for action. A wily enemy, the Japanese had made a mockery of open, above-board diplomacy. Stimson's man on the scene was Frank McCoy, who had gone to Manchuria with the Lytton Commission of the League of Nations and had confirmed the Japanese treachery. In 1905 Theodore Roosevelt, Stimson's hero of an earlier time, had negotiated a Russo-Japanese sphere of influence peace in Manchuria which had allowed for the continuation of American interests. The Portsmouth compromises, which divided spheres of influence, were now defunct. The Great Depression prevented any further American action at this time.

When Franklin Delano Roosevelt became President in 1933, he brought to power a more receptive ear and an internationalist's view. Arthur Schlesinger, Jr., has remarked that, even with the American domestic crises at the time, Roosevelt kept his thoughts on the foreign scene. Influencing Roosevelt from New York was Stimson and from Harvard was Frankfurter. Frankfurter acted as a recruiter of lawyers for government service and, at times, in the crisis, the usual internship for lawyers at Wall Street was bypassed. Roosevelt, in his speeches, cautiously geared the country for the war to come. The Pacific could not remain an American lake for long, as Japan began cutting off the China markets. In time the Atlantic lake was threatened by the militancy of Fascist Italy and Nazi Germany. Under Stimson's and Frankfurter's tutelage, America was to shed its isolationism by 1939.

Another figure linking eras of foreign-policy thought at this time was Douglas MacArthur, who was chief of staff of the army under both Hoover and Roosevelt from 1928 to 1936. MacArthur, as a military-political figure, might have been President in the tradition of the Harrisons, had he not divorced in 1929 the daughter of the founding Cromwell of the law firm of Sullivan and Cromwell. In 1936 MacArthur returned to the Philippines to build an army and an independent bastion against further Japanese encroachments toward Southeast Asia.

In 1940 Henry L. Stimson returned to the War Department, almost thirty years after his initial service there, to push for a hard-line policy toward the Japanese. The Hay-Root Open Door policy was defunct; an oil and steel embargo on Japan was begun. Stimson returned Harvey Bundy to the War Department, and with Bundy came his precocious son McGeorge Bundy, who had already written of the European threat to American security. Another Frankfurter-Stimson protégé was Dean Acheson, whose daughter later married Harvey Bundy's son William. George Marshall, a General Pershing protégé and an excellent product of the general staff system instituted by Stimson, became chief of staff. Marshall had been a staff planner in Europe during World War I, winning a general's star. After World War I, Marshall toured the staff colleges and grew knowledgeable about soldiers who might fight future wars. Marshall's black book is famous, for it contained the names of future American generals. Others, such as Second Lieutenant George Patton, who had known Stimson from his earlier War Department days, were viewed with favor.

In 1940 France and Holland fell and England was threatened; Southeast Asia was potentially a pushover for the Japanese, who were now in North Vietnam. America, alone at this point, could possibly preserve the colonial sphere of influence and the natural resources of this area. American national interest, which had previously concentrated on China, now brought into its concern Vietnam, Malaya, the Dutch East Indies, and Burma. Stimson also introduced a general staff system into foreign-policy planning. The Secretary of War visited universities throughout the country to involve Ph.D.'s in planning national policy over a longer-range period than previously. A center at Yale was established for this purpose. Some of the Ph.D.'s or Ph.D. candidates were siphoned into the OSS (the prototype CIA). Very bright individuals such as Walter Rostow became definers of national interest in this manner. At the end of World War II Walter Rostow continued as a State Department planner for national security affairs—an early version of the National Security Council which he was to head twenty years later.

Henry Stimson, still angered at the Japanese, hoped to deny them Southeast Asia. McGeorge Bundy's biography of Henry Stimson, *On Active Duty in Peace and War*, offers a good description of Stimson during this time. In 1940 Stimson drew a line in Vietnam at the 17th parallel, which the Japanese were informed they could not cross without provoking war. Because Hanoi had been lost as a major shipping point to China, the United States now hoped to use Cam Ranh Bay as a substitute. In 1939 Chennault's Flying Tigers had begun shipping planes through Hanoi. The Japanese ended this by seizing North Vietnam. Cam Ranh Bay was located below the 17th parallel and had been used by the Russians in 1905 to refuel their fleet on its way to fight the Japanese in the Pacific. FDR cautioned Stimson that the American public would not fight for Southeast Asia. When Pearl Harbor occurred, Henry Stimson was able to cry sneak attack and arouse the American public. He was thus able to vent his anger on the Japanese and end Japan's newly won hegemony in the Pacific, as well as build the American naval bases that were to preserve peace in the Pacific, as envisioned earlier by Alfred Thayer Mahan. Now that the Pacific was to become an American lake, it was necessary to make the Atlantic secure and to reduce Germany's influence.

Stimson realized that at his advanced age he could no longer carry forward the traditions he had come to represent. He therefore fostered postwar centralization programs that would institutionalize decision-making policies concerning American national interest. In 1947, an outgrowth of the OSS, the CIA, was created to centralize information gathering. At the same time the Department of Defense was organized to centralize war policy planning. Stimson's dream for a unified Defense Department came to fruition under James Forrestal, a Wall Street lawyer. Later the National Security Council was built, including representatives from the State Department, the CIA, and Department of Defense. Into the chairmanship of this council would come the true heirs of the Harrison tradition. Before the National Security Council was created, Stimson was able to continue influencing national policy through individuals who had performed well for him during World War II. Academicians such as Walter Rostow and Dean Rusk rose in a State Department run by George C. Marshall and Dean G. Acheson. Marshall later became the Secretary of Defense. No secrets were kept from Stimson and his heirs. Rather, it was Henry L. Stimson who first told President Harry S. Truman that an atomic bomb existed. When Truman had been Vice President he had not known of the atomic bomb.

At the end of the Stimson era under Democratic presidents, it was in the national interest to maintain the Pacific and Atlantic as American lakes ringed by naval and air bases on both sides of the oceans. It was also in the national interest to deny access to these areas to European or Pacific powers. Policy planning before World War II concentrated on Germany as the European power and Japan as the Asiatic power. Without much change in policy, it was simple to substitute Russia for Germany and Communist China for Japan as those nations most threatening to American national interest. To the traditional policy planners, the potential threat of Russia and China was enough to speed the institutionalization and centralization of foreign-policy axioms.

In 1953 John Foster Dulles, another of the Harrison traditionalists, became Secretary of State. Dulles had been a leading partner and administrator in the firm of Sullivan and Cromwell in the 1920s. During the 1930s his numerous books on foreign affairs discussed the need for a larger American presence in the world. Like his brother, Allen Dulles, John Foster Dulles was an internationalist. By 1940 he had become associated with Thomas E. Dewey. During World War II, Dulles acted as shadow-cabinet Republican secretary of state, thus helping to formulate a bipartisan posture during the war. Dulles attended the San Francisco United Nations meetings and the first General Assembly meetings. Dulles's ties to Dewey were rewarded by an appointment to the United States Senate. Foreign affairs remained Dulles's forte, and he left the Senate to negotiate along with Douglas MacArthur a Japanese Peace Treaty in 1951. A presidential boomlet for MacArthur followed but failed in 1952. A former MacArthur aide in the Philippines and a George Marshall protégé, General Dwight David Eisenhower, was to become the Republican nominee for President that year.

Under Eisenhower the institutionalization of national interest was personified by the Dulles brothers, one in the State Department and the other in the CIA. Allen Dulles had entered the OSS in 1940; he left the CIA in 1961 after nine years of his leadership. The Dulles brothers continued American interest in world order, in a strong military, and in an Atlantic and Pacific peace which had been institutionalized in economic and military multilateral treaties. John Foster Dulles's writings show the craftsmanship of a lawyer in search of the legitimization of world stability and peace. As a pragmatist he carried on the now traditional American spheres of influence.

The 17th parallel in Vietnam was maintained as a boundary in the 1954 Geneva Conference on Indochina. Dulles spoke of the necessity for maintaining friendly sea bases in Vietnam (Cam Ranh Bay) as well as friendly air routes over southern Indochina in order to maintain American hegemony in the Pacific-Southeast Asian theater. The untimely death of John Foster Dulles was not followed by a long hiatus in foreign-policy thinking, because a Democratic victory in 1960 returned to Washington the Harrison-Stimson heirs—McGeorge Bundy, Walt Rostow, and Dean Rusk—all aided by the voice of Dean Acheson in the background.

The quagmire of Vietnam can now be interpreted in the traditional context of what constitutes American national interest.

Lyndon Johnson has spoken of Vietnam as the end result of many wrong decisions by numerous functionaries of the bureaucracy. This attempt to rewrite history fails in light of Vietnam being a conscious decision by a small group of policy makers. It is no coincidence that our twice governor-general in Vietnam was Henry Cabot Lodge, whose father sat as a member of the foreign-policy planning elite under Benjamin Harrison. Others in the small, select group also played out semitraditional roles. By 1965 Lyndon Johnson saw himself as Franklin Delano Roosevelt, McGeorge Bundy as Henry Stimson, and Dean Rusk as George Marshall. Again, as in 1940 and 1954, the 17th parallel was to be preserved. In turn, Southeast Asia was to prosper under American might and hegemony. China was the expansionist power in Asia that Japan had once been. It was easy to view the attack at Pleiku as a parallel to the sneak attack at Pearl Harbor, and it was even easier to decide that the 17th parallel, now enshrined in American foreign-policy thinking, could not be crossed by either the Japanese, Chinese, or North Vietnamese. With these perceptions, the institutionalized response was to gear for war in Vietnam.

Individuals have wondered if the decision to enter Vietnam was based on personal economic interests. One doubts that any of the individuals of the Harrison tradition who were responsible for American escalation in Vietnam were either wealthy or had significant interests beyond what they believed to be American interests. The Bundys, Achesons, Rusks, Rostows, and others only maintained traditional policies created by prior generations of their Whig forebears. They see America still as needing to fight foreign wars as far from American shores as possible and as needing to maintain lines of communication to foreign markets. The relative smallness of the group of individuals who determined American foreign policy allowed a trusteeship over national interest to exist for almost two hundred years. The trust involved is an intellectual exercise rather than an economic interest.

A recent inheritor of this trust is Henry Kissinger. The Harvard riots of spring, 1969, unearthed McGeorge Bundy's 1957 letter of recommendation for the elevation of Henry Kissinger to the policy-planning councils. In 1957-58, Kissinger chaired a conference on national interest and wrote a book, *The Necessity of Choice*, summarizing the conference. This document became Kennedy's basic posture from 1961 through 1963.

Kissinger was to succeed John Foster Dulles as the leading foreign-policy advisor to the New York Republican Party. As Rockefeller's foreign-policy advisor and Dulles's heir, it was easy for Kissinger to move into Nixon's administration into an institutionalized position. In *A World Restored*, Henry Kissinger, giving credit to McGeorge Bundy, created an operative theory on the nature of peace and war. For a model, Kissinger used the post-Napoleonic stability which, created by the European powers, lasted through the revolutions of 1848. Like Metternich, Canning, and Talleyrand, Kissinger saw himself as maintaining the balance of power among existing great powers. His book provides interesting reading in a traditionalist world of stability and legitimacy threatened by revolutionary forces. Kissinger, as the latest trustee of the Whig tradition, has the role of deciding national goals within past frameworks.

By approaching the concept of national interest in terms of those who actually defend this interest, I feel one can come to a better understanding of past and present goals. It is important to understand the whims of as well as the pressures on individuals such as Stimson and Rostow if one is to gain insight into the nature of American foreign policy. Intensive study of Stimson's Rainbow Plan Five or Rostow's Plan Six as the policy doctrine for World War II and Vietnam is perhaps less fruitful than the study of Stimson and Rostow themselves and their roles in history.

We have outlined the long line of individuals who have contributed to present-day definitions of American national interest. Actual studies of these people are limited. Knowledge of these individuals allows one to understand traditional responses and to perhaps compose innovative answers to such problems as Vietnam. By defining how national policy has been structured, we may reach an understanding of the military-political implications of America's role in maintaining a future foreign policy which meets the needs of America and (hopefully) the world.

CHART I

AMERICAN NATIONAL INTEREST / THE INTERPRETERS

HARRISON TRADITION	ASSOCIATED POLITICAL ADVISORS	MILITARY-POLITICAL ADVISORS	THE PRESIDEN ADVISED
Benjamin Harrison (father) 1775-1787	James Wilson 1775-1798 John Tyler (father)	George Washington 1775-1799 Daniel Morgan 1775-1787 Anthony Wayne 1775-1796	Continental Con- gress George Washingt
William Henry Harrison (son) 1794-1841	John Tyler (son) 1836-1841	William Henry Harrison (son) 1794-1841	John Adams Thomas Jefferson James Madison James Monroe John Quincy Ada William Henry Harrison

(Note: Harrison and Tyler as the loyal opposition to Andrew Jackson and Martin Van Buren, 1829–1841)

John Tyler (son) 1841-1862	John Scott Harrison (grandson) to 1857	Zachary Taylor 1845-1848 Winfield Scott 1845-1861 (Military Whigs)	John Tyler James Polk Zachary Taylor Millard Fillmore Franklin Pierce

(Note: Tyler as a Whig leader in loyal opposition to James Buchanan, 1857–1861)

Benjamin Harrison (great-grandson) 1861-1901	James Garfield Andrew Johnson 1861-1865	George Henry Thomas (brother-in-law of Tyler) 1860-1869 Emory Upton 1865-1880 James Harrison Wilson 1861-1923	Abraham Lincoln Andrew Johnson U. S. Grant R. B. Hayes James Garfield C. A. Arthur
Benjamin Harrison 1889-1901	John Foster Theodore Roosevelt William Taft Alfred Mahan Henry Cabot Lodge	James Harrison Wilson	Benjamin Harrison

(Note: Benjamin Harrison as the loyal opposition to Grover Cleveland)

(continued

HARRISON TRADITION	ASSOCIATED POLITICAL ADVISORS	MILITARY-POLITICAL ADVISORS	THE PRESIDENT ADVISED
James Harrison Wilson 1901-1923	Elihu Root 1898-1912	Leonard Wood 1898-1928 Arthur MacArthur 1863-1907	William McKinley Theodore Roosevelt
Henry Stimson 1911-1913	Felix Frankfurter 1911-1913	Leonard Wood 1898-1928	William Howard Taft

(Note: Roosevelt, Stimson and Wood as the loyal opposition to Woodrow Wilson)

Robert Lansing 1915-1920	Felix Frankfurter 1915-1920	John J. Pershing 1916-1940	Woodrow Wilson
Herbert Hoover 1921-1932 Henry Stimson 1929-1932 1940-1945	Harvey Bundy John Foster Dulles (grandson John Foster, nephew Robert Lansing) 1940-1952 Allen Dulles 1940-1952 Felix Frankfurter	George Marshall 1918-1948 Douglas MacArthur 1911-1951	Warren Harding Calvin Coolidge Herbert Hoover Franklin Delano Roosevelt
Dean Acheson 1948-1952	The Dulles Brothers	George Marshall 1948-1950	Harry Truman
John Foster Dulles 1953-1959	Allen Dulles 1953-1961	Omar Bradley Matthew Ridgeway	Dwight Eisenhower
McGeorge Bundy (son Harvey Bundy) 1961-1965 William Bundy (brother of McGeorge— married Acheson's daughter) 1961-1968	Dean Acheson 1961-1968 Dean Rusk 1961-1968 Walter Rostow 1961-1968 Henry Cabot Lodge 1961-1968	Maxwell Taylor 1961-1969 Earl Wheeler 1961-1970	John Kennedy
The Bundy Brothers 1963-1968 Walter Rostow 1965-1968	Dean Acheson Dean Rusk	Maxwell Taylor	Lyndon Johnson
Henry Kissinger 1969-	The Bundy Brothers 1969- Dean Acheson	Maxwell Taylor	Richard Nixon Gerald Ford

SECTION III / THE CONCEPT OF THE ELITE ARMY UNIT

History gives scant credit to the presence of elite military units throughout the ages. Even less attention is given to what constitutes an elite fighting unit. Democracy fosters the concept that the citizen-soldier enlists (reluctantly), bears arms, wins wars and comes home to the laurels of the civilian population (Cincinnatus to Dwight Eisenhower). Military history is a subject receiving brief academic attention. Uncommonly do professors of military textbooks go to any depth in studying history's elite units.

In trying to understand why little attention is given to elite military units in history, the answer becomes clear that an elite unit does not exist without an elite general who has thought enough to create a unit which will later prove invincible on the battlefield. For those who command and will command, lessons about strategy must be complemented with lessons about the creation of an elite unit which will fight magnificently in battle. Following are some of the factors involved in creating elite units and a historical review and comparison of these various units.

The first unit, Gideon's, is Biblical in origin. Gideon gathered together the host of Israel to face the marauding Midianites. Thirty-two thousand Israelites responded to the call. The Lord spoke to Gideon and admonished him for the large size, so Gideon allowed those who didn't want to fight to go home. This left ten thousand men. A second message from the Lord repeated that there were too many, and a psychological test was devised to test those who were unfit for battle. In this test, the then thirsty men were sent to the water, and those who stood to watch for the enemy were picked out to fight. Only three hundred were left to fight the coming battle, which turned out to be a short night fight in which, by surprise and loud noises, the three hundred men of Gideon went among the camps of the Midianites creating confusion and forcing the Midianites to flee from the field.

Alexander's King's Companions was another elite unit. Alexander had taken 35,000 Macedonian troops across the Aegean and attacked the empire of Darius the Great. Among his troops was a group called the King's Companions, a group of 300 heavy cavalry. These were friends of the king, who trained with him for a number of years and later proved their mettle in battle. Their most significant victory came when Darius lined up all his troops, six hundred thousand or more, against the 35,000 Greeks. The 300 members of the King's Companions darted from the rear of the army's phalanx and headed straight for the center of the Persian line behind which stood Darius and his standard. The Companions broke through the center, Darius fled, and the Persian army retreated from the field. This does not demean the steadiness of the Greek phalanx, but the success in surprise, the concept of the small number, and the superior mobility of the cavalry all allowed for the feeling of invincibility of Alexander as he marched to the Indus River. From his King's Companions Alexander chose those who would marry Persian women in his humanitarian belief in the brotherhood of man.

Julius Caesar as ruler of Spain and Gaul also had the chance to raise a legion to his liking. This was his Tenth Legion, which he equipped and trained, winning victories in Gaul, England, Spain, and later in Italy. The size of the legion was approximately 6,000 men. It was a stalwart force, used mostly in reserve, but it was highly mobile and able to be at the scene of battle in crucial moments.

An elite unit was instrumental in the great conquests of Ghenghis Khan, and one need look no further than the Mongol Captain Sabutai and his cavalry unit, the touman. His forces utilized speed, surprise, maneuverability, and an improved communications system to capture Korea, Japan, Russia, Poland, and Hungary. Sabutai's cavalry touman and two other toumans in Europe were able to leave more than 97,000 Polish and Hungarian troops dead on the battlefield in Hungary. Sabutai's troops were cavalrymen who had developed flag signals for use in battle. These flag signals, transmitted to the "blind" Sabutai, allowed the leader to determine the course of battle. The Mongols' speed on the march, their ability to use surprise, and the fear with which they were regarded allowed a small number of men to conquer an empire from Japan to Hungary. During the summer the men of Sabutai were on long military jaunts, and in the winter they trained for the summer to come.

In the Thirty Years' War between 1618 and 1648, Gustaphus Adolphus created a small, victorious, mobile elite unit. He mixed cavalry, pikemen and musketeers in checkerboard patterns in battle. Constantly moving, these squares created confusion among the homogeneous forces that faced them. A comparable elite army of the time was Oliver Cromwell's Parliamentary Army. At its height between 1645 and 1650, Cromwell and 20,000 highly trained and well-equipped men pacified Britain, Ireland and Scotland. His men, referred to as "Ironsides" and "Roundheads," developed a cavalry able to match and defeat the forces of the Royal Cavalry.

Frederick the Great brings to mind the elite Prussian grenadiers. Their training made them capable of firing three times faster than any other army in the field. Frederick, using small numbers of troops compared to the combined forces of Austria, Russia and France, was still able to hold off the allies. After many wars Frederick controlled far larger boundaries than those with which he had started, leaving the legacy upon which modern Germany was built. But it was not among his grenadiers that the elite force existed. Rather, it was his cavalry, which has been overlooked. This cavalry was under the command of Seydlitz, and many victories are attributable to the speed, maneuverability, and decisive actions taken in battle by Seydlitz's cavalry in coordination with larger numbers of infantry.

The *levee-en-masse*, beginning with the French Revolution, caused generals to forgo the small elite unit. Due to the new, superior firepower of the common soldier, the uncommon soldier was to give way to the large army of the citizen-soldier. But the lessons of Napoleon in Russia, Grant in Virginia, and the Germans at Verdun attested to the futility of the conscripted soldier in action when pressed beyond his innate ability to defend his homeland. Even in World War II the early mass levees of the American Army met defeat in Africa at the Kasserine Pass as well as in the Philippines in 1941-42.

The citizen-soldier in the wars of the nineteenth and twentieth centuries has often received credit for victories—credit which belonged instead to whichever side had taken the time and patience to create a modern elite force. Napoleon did try to create an elite unit in his Old Guard, but it was used more often in reserve and as a façade. Instead, Davout, one of Napoleon's finest generals, created the fighting force that was able to protect Napoleon's rear-guard in the Russian retreat and to control large territories. Without Davout and his first corps present in 1814-15, Napoleon lost his empire. Perhaps Napoleon's greatest victories can be ascribed to the talents of Davout and his force of well-trained men. In one action, Davout, with a force of perhaps 20,000 men, met and defeated an Austro-Hungarian force of 70,000 men. Had Davout been present at Leipzig and at Waterloo, perhaps the course of battle would have gone differently. One then looks to Napoleon's victor, Wellington, to find an elite unit. In the peninsular campaign and at Waterloo were the King's German Legion, a highly mobile, disciplined fighting force. This is not to take credit from the Scottish, Irish, English, Spanish, and Portuguese soldiers who had fought valiantly with Wellington but rather to point out that within Wellington's army was a singular elite cavalry unit.

Turning to American history, it is no harder to find an elite unit in the first 90 years of our history. Perhaps one had begun almost before the revolution. These were the Virginia soldiers under Daniel Morgan. They had fought in campaigns against the Indians in 1774 and 1775 in West Virginia. Later they went to

Boston to be sent up the Kennebec River with Benedict Arnold in an attempt to capture Quebec. In a howling snowstorm the troops of Morgan and Arnold, 300 Virginians and 600 New Englanders, combined with another force from New York and were able to capture the lower city but were beaten at the last moment in the inner city of Quebec. This elite force, which had just gotten started, was thus decimated and captured. Arnold and Morgan again combined their talents at Freeman's Farm to win the decisive victory of Saratoga. Daniel Morgan can be further credited with the finest colonial victory of the war at Cowpens in a Cannae-type battle using regulars and militia.

During the American Civil War, General George Henry Thomas took time to create the backbone of the Army of the Cumberland. In contrast to the enormous casualties of the Army of the Potomac, the Army of the Cumberland became a veteran, well-trained, unbeatable fighting force. After two years of training and various battles, the army was able to commit itself fully at the Battle of Missionary Ridge in Chattanooga in 1863, opening the gateway to the South. The same Army of the Cumberland fought to Atlanta, brilliantly outmaneuvering Confederate General Johnson before taking Atlanta. Sherman took the Army of the Cumberland away from Thomas and marched to Savannah and then northward. This unit, perhaps 60,000 strong at its height in the siege of Atlanta, received very little credit for its exceptional fighting ability. But Thomas, even without his army, was still able to win the greatest battle of the Civil War in cooperation with James Harrison Wilson. In 1863 Wilson created the Cavalry Command in Washington. In 1864 he regrouped and took command of the Cavalry of the West, keeping the number of soldiers in his major units under ten thousand. At the Battle of Nashville, Thomas utilized Wilson's cavalry to win a victory in which 32,000 of General Hood's Confederate soldiers were destroyed. The First Brigade of Wilson's Cavalry Command under Emory Upton later destroyed the troops of Nathan Bedford Forrest at Selma, Alabama. In the Union Army were both a cavalry command and an infantry force which deserved the title "elite." What Grant's legions could not effectively do head-on against Lee's army in Virginia, the much smaller armies of Thomas and Wilson were able to do to the rear of the Confederate forces by destroying the remaining units of the Confederate armies of the West. Certainly this was no mean feat in enemy territory.

At Caporetto in Italy, at Riga in Latvia, and in the 1918 campaign of the German army in France, small unit tactics were devised. At Caporetto an infantry captain named Erwin Rommel trained his German troops to go on top of the mountain ridges, to get behind the unsuspecting Italian forces, creating havoc and panic which led to the decimation of more than half a million Italian soldiers. In 1917 in Riga, Jaeger elite forces were first used and later they were employed more successfully on the French front in 1918.

It is not until the Russian Revolution that we find the recreation of an elite fighting unit under Vasily Bleucher. In 1918 he formed the Iron Division to sweep from the Urals, defeating Admiral Kolchak, and to sweep to the Crimea, defeating General Deniken. Bleucher then conquered Siberia. Between 1921 and 1923 he developed the Siberian Army, which was able to drive the French, the Americans, the Japanese, the Czechs, the British, the Cossacks, and other White Russian forces out of Siberia. He built a fighting force which effectively conquered one of the largest areas of the world. Bleucher then went to China to train the Kuomintang army commanders. He also indoctrinated the Chinese Communist officer corps and, in time, it was the Chinese Eighth Route Army which was the vital factor in the success of the Chinese Communists. This army was placed under the leadership of Lin Piao, who brought the vanguard troops out of the trap laid by Chiang Kai-shek in 1933. Lin Paio's troops, with their mobility, small numbers, and capacity for surprise, led the major body of the Communist army through the Long March. In 1937 Lin Piao's forces were the first to defeat the Japanese in battle. In 1945 he was able to take this Eighth Route Army, then estimated at more than 50,000 men, into Manchuria, completely controlling the province by 1948, to continue marching into Peking, and by 1950, to march to the sea and Hainan Island in Southern China.

Other elite units formed during World War II were the New Zealand Division and the Ghurka Division which formed part of Montgomery's British Eighth Army, the Desert Army. Field Marshal Montgomery took the time to train the British Eighth Army effectively in the desert. The emphasis on night maneuvers and on coordinating the infantry with the new mechanized tactics of fighting, when linked with the patience to await battle until victory was assured, led to El Alamein and the crushing of Rommel's Afrika Korps in Tunis.

The military lessons of the centuries indicate that an outstanding elite unit must be built and maintained for the pursuit of war. The peasant army, the regional army, the phalanx, the *levee-en-masse*, were actually the foundations from which the generals trained the smaller permanent elite fighting units.

What factors went into creating the elite units so that generals would not forget the lessons of the past? First, the unit had to be homogeneous. Homogeneity could be achieved by picking men from the same background: the Mongols of Sabutai, the Macedonians of Alexander, the Spanish troops of Caesar, the English troops of Cromwell. Homogeneity could also be achieved by screening.

Second, it took two years to properly train an elite unit before it could be committed effectively to victories on the battlefield. Until that time, it was a defensive fighting unit. Third, it had to be of small size. It could range anywhere from 300 to 60,000, but between 6,000 and 10,000 troops was probably optimal.

Above are detailed comparisons of elite units in history. In addition, the political consequences of the *continued* use of an elite unit are manifold. Alexander's King's Companions were able to survive and create the empires of the Seleucids, the Ptolemies, and the Macedonians. Caesar's legions were the groundwork for the Roman Empire which was to come. The legions of the Khan were able to maintain the Mongol dynasty for a hundred years. The legions of Thomas and Wilson produced political figures such as Benjamin Harrison, Andrew Johnson, James Garfield, Governor Cox of Ohio, and Governor Palmer of Illinois. The elite army created by Bleucher in Russia later became the salvation of Moscow when the Siberian Army troops were transferred from Vladivostok to Moscow in 1941. Next, the defense of Stalingrad relied on the Siberian Army. Lin Piao's Eighth Route Army has provided the stability of Communist China.

The military historian should seek to discover an elite unit and its role in the history of any nation which achieves great conquests. It is also important to view a great general, not as a single figure, but as part of the armies he created to win his victories. The future general should look to the tactical lessons of his predecessors to learn to utilize the principles of the elite unit in time to come.

PART III / THE CHINESE SPRING

INTRODUCTION

During the late 1960s the turmoil of modern China became daily reading fare. To many, China remained inexplicable. The question is to explain the social movements of other cultures in universal terms so that we may understand these phenomena. One must attempt to understand the role and interactions of Mao Tse-tung with the people of China to have a practical and realistic attitude toward China.

The second section, entitled "Yardsticks for Vietnam" (1965), can be read in the context of Bleucher in China as the teacher of Mao Tse-tung. I have also included a commentary on Lin Piao's "Long Live the Victory of the People's War" (1965). His broadside was interpreted as a declaration of war and thus was one of the reasons for his fall from power. By becoming an implacable foe of the United States, Lin Piao had removed a significant option from the foreign scene. He thus left the more flexible Chinese such as Chou En-lai to become the followers of Mao Tse-tung as China reached out to new strategies in the late 1960s and the early 1970s.

DRAMATIS PERSONAE

The Players (in some order of importance)

Mao Tse-tung, Chairman Chinese Communist Party (1893-1976)
Lin Piao, Field Commander of the Red Army (1907-1971)
Chen Yi, Field Commander of the Red Army (1901-1972)
Chou En-lai, close associate of Mao Tse-tung, premier
(1898-1976)
Chu Teh, close associate of Mao Tse-tung, general (1886-   )
Teng Hsiao P'ing, Field Commander of the Red Army
(1903-   )
Liu Po-ch'eng, Field Commander of the Red Army (1892-   )
Nieh Jung-chen, Field Commander of the Red Army (1899-   )
Liu Shao-chi, Communist party theoretician (1898-   )
Chiang Kai-shek, statesman (1886-1975)
Yuan Shih-K'ai, Chinese statesman (1859-1916)
Chen Chiung-ming, Bleucher's opponent in Canton (1875-1933)
Eugene Chen, Left Wing of Kuomintang (1878-1944)
Mikhail Markovich Borodin (Grusenberg), Soviet political advisor
of Chiang Kai-shek (1884-1953)
Chang Tso-Lin, Warlord of Manchuria (1873-1928)
Adolph Abrahamovich Joffe, Soviet political advisor of Sun Yat-
sen (1883-1927)
Chang Hsueh-liang, Warlord of Manchuria (1898-   )
Maksim Maksimovich Litvinov, Russian statesman (1876-1951)
Sun Yat-sen, physician, revolutionary (1866-1925)

KEY ACTS

Boxer Rebellion	1900
Chinese Revolution	1911
Sun Yat-sen requests Russian advisors	1923
Chiang Kai-shek leads the Northern March	1926-1928
Nanchang Red Revolt and Autumn Harvest Revolt	August 1, 1927
Japanese Invasion of Manchuria	1931
Mao Tse-tung leads all of Mainland China	1934-1937
Sino-Japanese War begins	July 7, 1937
VJ Day	September 2, 1945
Mao Tse-Tung leads all of Mainland China	1949
Korean War	1950-1953
French-Viet Minh War	1945-1954
United States and Indochina	1954-1975

SECTION I / A COMMENTARY ON "LONG LIVE THE VICTORY OF THE PEOPLE'S WAR"

Simply stated, on September 2, 1965, Marshal Lin Piao, minister of defense of Red China, in "Long Live the Victory of the People's War," accepted the inevitability of war with the United States. For an appropriate interpretation of this action, we must recognize that in the major capitals of the Communist world, Peking and Moscow, there are war parties as well as peace parties. The aims and policies of each of these capitals are debated by these two factions as are the methods and means of accomplishing various tasks. In Moscow they are the right-wing evolutionists versus the left-wing revolutionists (Kosygin and Brezhnev versus Suslov and Shelepin). In Peking the division has been between the hard-line Chinese Communist party apparatus represented by Teng Hsiao-p'ing, the secretary general of the party, and Peng Cheng, the mayor of Peking (who date their party loyalties from the Long March in 1934-36 under Mao Tse-tung), and the soft-line members of the Politburo represented by the military generals (who date their party membership before or during their training by the Russians at the Whampoa Military Academy in 1926 and by their having raised the flag of the Chinese Communist rebellion on August 1, 1927, at Nanchang, China). The soft liners have been Chou En-lai, Chen Yi, Lin Piao, and other marshals of the Chinese hierarchy; they have been more willing to accept a slower (rightist) approach to eventual Communist victory and in the past were more likely to accept the reasoning of the post-Khrushchev Soviet leadership as to a policy of moderation toward the United States.

However, since Khrushchev's fall, the pro-Russian Chinese Communists have apparently been rebuked by, and clashed with, the new Soviet leadership. The first soft liner to undergo a change of attitude was Chou En-lai. In visiting Moscow late in 1964, Chou En-lai was unable to change Soviet attitudes toward India or Indonesia. Chou accepted the fact that the Soviet position would continue to be unrealistic in terms of the Chinese view of the world. Chou then attempted to undermine the Soviet influence in Africa and Asia. Chen Yi, in rapid political forays into Indonesia and Pakistan, again established that American, Soviet, and Chinese intentions in Asia clashed.

Lin Piao's 20,000 word document marks Lin's conversion to the hard-line view of the inevitability of a Sino-American conflict. Lin appears finally convinced that the United States is "clamoring" for a trial of strength with the Chinese people and for another large-scale ground war on the Asian mainland. As a military man, Lin finds the United States to have overreached itself, to have stretched its supply lines, and to have dispersed its strength. Militarily, Lin finds the moment for war most propitious as China can launch diversionary "people's wars" in Asia, Africa, and Latin America, as well as on its own borders which, as limited protracted wars, will further stretch American supply lines. In making his decision, he denies the utilization or effectiveness of nuclear weapons as influencing the course of a future war, for Lin will defend neither cities nor fixed points. Politically, Lin believes that moral force has entered the arena on his side, through the "aggressive" commitment of United States troops in South Vietnam. Lin also interprets the political conscience of the Asian peoples as recognizing American blunders in the muddled, cross-cultural Asian waters. Lin Piao is then an important Chinese figure from the Chinese side of the doves to move to the side of the war hawks. *This is the meaning of the document: Lin has placed himself on record as declaring war on the United States.*

Lin Piao ranks as one of the top living generals in the world today. All successful Chinese Communist military tactics were evolved under his leadership. Reputedly, he has never lost a battle. Trained by the Russians, Lin was an honor graduate of their school at Whampoa in Canton. He was a Kuomintang colonel at age eighteen and a Chinese Communist general at age nineteen. He quickly won the reputation of having been victorious in a hundred battles without defeat. Mao Tse-tung's military writings were interpreted by Lin Piao when Lin was the commandant of the Yunnan Chinese Communist Military Academy in the 1930s. He has taught and influenced face to face the second-generation Chinese Communist military leadership. In addition, in 1937 Lin won the first Chinese "United Front" battle against the Japanese south of Peking and destroyed the myth of Japanese invincibility. In 1945, Lin infiltrated 50,000 Eighth Route Army men into Manchuria, where he re-formed the Eighth Route Army and where, with the help of Rodion Y. Malinovsky, he re-equipped the army with Japanese weapons. Marshal Malinovsky also taught Lin Piao the secrets of city fighting. After 1945 the Chinese Communists changed from guerrilla tactics in rural areas to positional warfare in the cities. The "short attack," developed at Stalingrad, was the tactical lesson Lin Piao learned from the Soviets. Lin's victory in the cities of Manchuria was followed by a successful sweep to the southern tier of China.

In 1950, Lin Piao launched the Eighth Route Army (4th Field Army) against the United Nations forces across the Yalu. The men of the Eighth Route Army drove their opponents back to the 38th parallel. A second winter-spring offensive drove the United Nations forces even farther south. Lin was then transferred to Southern China in response to the need to prepare for a possible second front across the Formosa Straits from Taiwan. In 1959 Lin Piao became minister of defense of Communist China. A shadowy figure, often fictitiously sick, Lin Piao has avoided the limelight and the forefront of major power struggles.

Lin is a general whose thinking about guerrillas, flank attacks, concentration of forces, and retreats when necessary, is reminiscent of the thinking of Frederick the Great and Marshal Gebhard Blücher. Lin Piao's thinking matches that of Frederick the Great in Prussia in 1740-45 and 1755-63. Lin is oriented to wars against more powerfully equipped armies, just as Frederick, with interior lines, faced the armies of France, Austria, and Russia. Fighting for forty years as a warrior for an inferior power, Lin has little fear of other armies in a major war.

In my opinion, Lin is the deepest of the Chinese military-political thinkers and an individual who, next to Mao Tse-tung, carries the most weight in China in doctrinaire military-political battles. For Western Sinologists to pass over Lin Piao's document as a repetition of previous doctrine or as fluff or as an ebb-tide device is unwarranted. The document represents the analytical thoughts of a top Communist leader who has humbly struggled to reach a decision, a decision for war.

SECTION II / YARDSTICKS FOR VIETNAM: A REVIEW OF FIVE TWENTIETH-CENTURY MILITARY-ASSISTANCE MISSIONS

Over forty years ago Soviet Russia and Germany provided political and military assistance as well as technical training to feed the fires of internal revolutions. These military missions were: (1) Soviet Russia to Outer Mongolia, 1921-24; (2) Soviet Russia to China, 1923-27; (3) Germany to China, 1928-36; (4) Soviet Russia to Spain, 1937-39; and (5) Germany to Spain, 1936-39. In the article, Soviet Russia and Germany are referred to as helping nations, and China, Spain, and Outer Mongolia are called host nations. By questioning and studying the efforts of each mission, tactics can be learned and applicable conclusions can be drawn. These conclusions can then be compared individually by the reader to the military mission in Vietnam. The reader can then develop his own yardsticks for success or failure of the internal wars of the 1960s.

The specter of Communist or Nazi political ideology which overhangs these missions has often led Americans not to appreciate these earlier missions. Time can allow the viewing of individual tactics of those military missions as their most important feature. When these military tactics are isolated for scrutiny, comparisons can be made. These comparisons allow for analysis.

Today, American military missions are assigned to help nations undergoing the stress of transitional development. Yesterday's lessons could be that much more applicable in planning tomorrow's military missions.

Question I:

When is the most likely time that a host country will request a military mission?

Newly emerging nations attempt first to provide their own leadership and to modernize by themselves. If the nation is then unable to achieve stability, the initial period of national self-confidence and pride is followed by a cry for help by segments of the population.

The three host nations each had major revolutions against their traditional pasts at least five years prior to requests for help. These revolutions occurred in Outer Mongolia in 1911, China in 1911, and Spain in 1931. These revolutionary breaks with social institutions and traditions of the past had led to frustrations as well as failures. In the frustrating stage of transition into modern statehood, many difficulties led to the recognition by a few of the country's need for help. Neither Germany nor Russia offered aid immediately to the host countries. However, segments of leadership within the host countries themselves evolved who chose to call upon specific nations for aid.

Question II:

What institution within the helping country has a major influence on the host country's choice of a helping nation to dispatch a military mission?

A decisive factor would seem to be open and freely encouraged university, college, and vocational facility enrollment policies of the helping countries toward the host countries. The foreign educational background of emerging host-country leadership provides a clue as to which country or countries would be asked to provide help.

Beginning in 1917, the Soviets were able to offer educational help to Outer Mongolians who sought further training. Leaders of the 1921 Soviet-supported Outer Mongolian Revolution, Sukhebator and Marshal Choibalsang, were both educated in Siberia. Even after the Outer Mongolian Revolution was successful, the Soviets continued to train Outer Mongolians as teachers and technicians to replace Soviet advisors supplied to Outer Mongolia.

Soviet leaders founded universities with enrollments specifically open to Asian pupils. Sun Yat-sen (Eastern Toilers) University in Moscow was to become a magnet for young Asians. Even Frunze (Moscow) Military Academy was open to foreign students. Enrollment at Frunze included two apt Spanish pupils, Juan Modesto and Enrique Lister, generals of the Spanish Loyalist cause. These universities in Moscow provided graduates to supply host-country factions with Soviet-leaning and Soviet-educated native leadership.

The Central European universities also provided opportunities for many Chinese and Spanish individuals to study and look toward the German model as an answer. The more famous of these universities were in Heidelberg and Berlin.

A tactic of allowing open university enrollment to educate personnel of developing nations seems to open the borders of the host country to a helping military mission.

Question III:

Which host-country personalities provide the key for making a success of a helping country's program in the political and military spheres?

The German and Russian military missions linked themselves to the *downward mobile* intelligentsia in order to ensure success, whether immediate or future. A description of downward mobility would be a present and future degrading of one's traditional elite social and economic position during the transitional years of turmoil which follow a break with past traditions. Individuals who have seen better times are more apt to be frustrated and to seek through new programs a chance to regain their traditional roles. Revolution thus becomes the opportunity to renew their status in society with a more modern meaning. Crisis is their time to regain past status, even to the point of martyrdom. More often than not, the downwardly mobile people are the scions of a former elite class, representing the educated or the native intelligentsia. Those who perceive themselves as having downward mobility are those who have worked hardest for economic and social revolutions and have often achieved success.

In Outer Mongolia the 1911 Revolution had enriched pro-Tsarist and later pro-White Russian merchants, priests, and princes; these groups no longer had to pay taxes to the Manchus of China. Soviet Russia aided the Mongolians who saw themselves as more oppressed by the victors of the 1911 Revolution than they had been by the Manchus. When the Soviet-advised Mongolians entered Ulan Bator in 1921, they removed the pro-White Russian merchants and limited the power of priests and princes. To replace the new 1911 ruling class, the Soviets elevated both Soviet-advised Mongolians and Chinese scribes who had been downgraded by the 1911 Revolution.

In China, sons of mandarins, small landholders, and small-factory owners flocked to Sun Yat-sen's Kuomintang. New large-scale Western industries and modern industrial ideas and technology had proved more damaging to these educated sons of the old elite than had the past years of empire. No niche was provided for many of the educated sons of the old mandarin classes in the new Western industrialization programs and factories. To gain relief from the ills of the transitional years, the more frustrated turned to progress offered by the Soviets.

Republican Spain, victorious in 1931, had constructed new systems for achieving elite status and for upward mobility. Official positions in the unions, in the militia, and in the major parties of Anarchists, Socialists, and Center Republicans now represented the upwardly mobile path toward leadership and elite status. In

Spain, downward mobility was found in the army, the church, and among the landholders. Germany aided the downwardly mobile who were most aware of their loss of status. The Russians aided a group of Spanish Republicans who could not submit their new status to the discipline required in war, a disadvantage the Russians did not overcome.

Question IV:

How is the loyalty of the key personnel (the downwardly mobile) maintained?

Appeals are made to the loyalty of the downwardly mobile by gearing them to the possibility of jobs in the "wave-of-the-future." Soviet ideology, perhaps even more than Western ideology, is able to appeal to the downwardly mobile intelligentsia (the old elite class) by promising jobs in the coming Marxist utopia. In fact, many unemployed intelligentsia are needed and are used to fulfill managerial responsibilities as well as teaching needs in a Marxist state.

Soviet policy in Mongolia replaced the so-called capitalistic traders in goods with the downwardly mobile intelligentsia. Scribes and literate people who had never deserted a pro-Russian attitude were given government positions upon the arrival of the Soviets; later these people were trained to handle agricultural farms and industries in Outer Mongolia.

Soviet policy in China utilized the downwardly mobile as faculty members and commissars of regiments. These teachers and commissars were to be the backbone of the Chinese and North Vietnamese Communist civil struggle and victory. Sons of mandarins, such as Chinese Premier Chou En-lai and North Vietnamese Premier Pham Van Dong, were representatives of an old elite class. These intellectuals were given responsibility. In return, they have been in the front of Communist struggles for the last forty years.

The failure of the Soviet tactics in Spain was perhaps related to the limited number of links which the Soviets were able to build between themselves and the native intelligentsia. Instead, the Soviets chose to bring pretrained, foreign, Communist, intellectual leadership from non-Spanish countries.

Rather than employ the new downwardly mobile, the Soviets chose to purge, discipline, and jail the cream of Loyalist Spain. Utilization of the Checka or OGPU in Spain drove the intellectuals away from the Soviets. Purges in Barcelona and Madrid reached potential supporters of a compromise Popular Front, such as Trotskyites (POUM) and Anarchists. In time, the panegyrists of Loyalist Spain, like Ernest Hemingway, were not to be Spanish. The bells had tolled for the non-Franco-leaning Spanish intellectuals.

Interestingly, the Germans in Spain and China could never find employment outside the army for the intelligentsia. The Germans never created a Chou En-lai or a Mao Tse-tung to immortalize the German way of life. Even in victory, Nazi philosophy did not take root in Spain, as Franco's *Corporate State* had been derived from Benito Mussolini and Italy. In China (Taiwan), Chiang Kai-shek's closest advisors had been trained by the Russians rather than by the Germans.

Question V:

Was there a tactic executed upon the arrival of a military mission that provided an initial clue to the ultimate success or failure of the mission?

This tactic appears to have been the founding of schools within the host country. The most famous of the early host-country schools was Whampoa Military and Political Academy in Canton, a local school financed by the Soviets. Within the school over 5,000 future Kuomintang and Chinese Communist officers were trained. Officially the faculty was 100 percent Asian, indirectly guided by Soviet advisors. The future faculty and students, whether Kuomintang or Communist at Whampoa, would continue looking to the Soviets for guidance in the military as well as other spheres. Chiang Kai-shek, who denounced the Chinese Communists in 1927, still allowed his son to be schooled in Moscow. From 1937 to 1942, Chiang reinvited a second Soviet military mission to China to train his armies. Later, the Chinese Communists were to seek Russian help from 1945 to 1956.

Local host-country schools were also founded by the Germans. They established the Nanking Central Academy and other technical schools. In Nationalist Spain the Germans created specialized technical schools to teach Spanish army officers and NCOs.

Soviet response in Spain was to attempt to develop massive elementary school educational programs to combat illiteracy. In avoiding the further training of the intelligentsia, the Soviets were not able to develop competent native political and military leaders.

Question VI:

Which methods of instruction and classroom format were most useful in developing successful host country leadership?

If Whampoa is appreciated as the true fountain of recent Kuomintang and Red Chinese leadership, then it would be valuable to dissect the methods of instruction to see their educational advantages. The most popular method of instruction was the seminar, which even then was a teaching tool. Problem-solving group discussions, utilizing the seminar method, aided in developing leadership skills of pupils and of participating faculty.

This indirect method of instruction, the seminar, was the most successful form of teaching at Whampoa. When competent Chinese educators could not be found, North Vietnamese and other Asians were brought in as teachers. Soviet advisors at Whampoa had only praise for the efforts of their Asian faculty members, whom they allowed to lead and teach. Mainland China and North Vietnam have been led by men whose abilities were developed at Whampoa in Canton. Those in attendance included Mao Tse-tung, Chou En-lai, Marshal Lin Piao, Marshal Chen Yi, Marshal Nieh Jung-chen, Hsu Hsiang-chen, Ho Chi Minh, Pham

Van Dong, and others. Few schools which lasted less than five years can boast of such graduates and faculty members.

Other classroom formats added to Whampoa's capacity to produce leadership. Whampoa was divided into a military and a political school. Individuals were not taught to be commanders or commissars but cross-trained as commander-commissars. The military and political sections were not seen as separate entities but rather as spheres of leadership, each an extension of the other. A graduate was a leader of men, not a specialist in a weapon or an inflexible idea. Both faculty and students could move from discussion to discussion, whether it was political or military. Immediate practical experience was provided for the classroom discussions in the streets of Canton and its immediate provinces, as civil disturbance revolved around the school. Generalists rather than specialists were trained at Whampoa, as the wide latitude of on-the-job experience allowed the students to develop their skills of leadership.

To emphasize the Asian role at Whampoa, the German-speaking head of the Soviet military mission, Vasily Bleucher, dressed as a native, ate Chinese food with relish and acted the Sinophile.

Another important lesson taught at Whampoa was that leadership was the essential message of the Soviet teachers. Politics and wars were seen as the arts of interpersonal and intergroup relationships. Soviet advisors strove by speech and by deed to build aggressive leadership within the Chinese. Bleucher's struggle to divorce flexible principles of leadership and thought from the inflexibilities of ideology was perhaps one aspect of Soviet success with the pupils of Whampoa, later the rulers of China and North Vietnam. In turn, leadership in these countries has shown the ability to stand on two feet, bowing to interpretations of communism neither from Moscow nor Peking.

The proving grounds for Whampoa had been the Rokossovsky-captained and Bleucher-directed military advisory mission to Outer Mongolia in 1921. Reputedly, this expedition consisted mainly of Soviet Buriat Mongol tribesmen who joined native Mongol revolutionaries at the border to capture Ulan Bator. The Soviets quickly moved in to a secondary role in Outer Mongolia, while the Soviet military mission trained a large Mongol army and lent it Soviet technical assistance.

Question VII:

What alternative methods of instruction were used to develop host country leadership?

An alternative method which proves successful over short periods of time is the founding of specialized military schools. In China the Germans established schools for each military branch: air force, navy, artillery, armor, etc. Chinese soldiers learned on German equipment and quickly mastered modern weaponry. Each school trained specialists who proved effective against Chinese Communist groups in the 1930s. However, Chiang's army of specialists performed relatively poorly during the 1937-45 Sino-Japanese conflict. Before they could conduct further military action, the specialists had to be retrained by the Soviet Union and the United States because of the change to Soviet and American equipment. In 1937, Vasily Chuikov, a Soviet instructor at Whampoa, replaced the German teachers.

In Spain the German effort to establish specialized military schools did provide Franco with a modern Spanish army in 1936. Subsequently, this army was tied to antiquated German arms and ammunition but did not have German-oriented leadership.

The German schools in Spain and China apparently developed followers rather than creative or even German-oriented leadership. Possibly the German schools were too successful in emphasizing the one-to-many relationship to "Herr Professor."

The Soviet Union chose not to develop native leadership in Civil War Spain but rather utilized pretrained foreign leadership, the International Brigade. Native Spanish antagonism toward foreign influence led to the removal of the International Brigade's leadership and finally the removal of the brigade from Spain. Ap-

131

parently because the Russians brought pretailored foreign-born leadership, the Soviets were unable to gain the support of the Spanish people.

Question VIII:

What role in the success or failure of the missions was played by the military equipment supplied by the helping countries?

The less heavy equipment brought into the host country, the better were the chances for the native leadership to learn about leadership rather than about heavy equipment only. In Spain, the Soviets and Germans had to maintain their armor and air force as well as locate personnel who could teach more than just technical usage of the weapons of war. Armor experts such as Konev, Malinovsky and Rokossovsky, all of World War II fame, were wasted in the hilly terrain of Spain. Small arms, rather than heavy equipment from the Soviets, saved the Outer Mongolian and Chinese revolutions; Mexican rifles that arrived in Madrid in 1936 bolstered the early Loyalist cause. This example stresses the Soviet success with rifles and propaganda in Mongolia in 1921 and in China in 1925, as contrasted with later Soviet and German efforts in China in 1937 and in Spain in 1936.

When advisors took the time to teach the use of planes, tanks, and large crew-serviced weapons, they were not able to teach host-country personnel the art of leadership. In this way advisors failed in their mission.

Question IX:

What are the goals of the successful military mission?

A successful mission attempts to limit its goals. When a mission comes to teach principles of war and principles of political leadership, the mission is able to accomplish these limited goals. When a mission comes to fight a war of principle, it is rarely successful.

In 1921-27 and 1937-42, Soviet military advisors at Ulan Bator, Whampoa, and Nanking attempted to limit themselves to the goal of building a native leadership corps. When members of the Soviet Political Mission to China (1926-27) attempted to fight a war of principle, both the political and the military missions failed. The chief Soviet political advisor, Mikhail Borodin, even attempted to build a Red Labor Army in Wuhan in Central China, without the help of the Soviet military in Canton. Borodin's efforts ended in the destruction of both the pro-Soviet army and Soviet-leaning Chinese government in 1927. Later, Chiang Kai-shek, the victor over the Wuhan group, wrote Stalin many times requesting Bleucher to train his troops and to replace or augment the German advisory mission.

Soviet goals in Spain overran the bounds of teaching the arts of leadership and the principles of the battlefield. Instead, the Soviets tried to force a Communist conformity which drove many potential Spanish recruits away from a pro-Soviet orbit. So-called civilian political experts attempted, by blind faith and pride in communism, to stifle the more practical individual initiative and self-confidence. There has been no Mao Tse-tung in Spain to carry on the Soviet influence.

Germany, in both China and Spain, limited its goals to building an officer corps. By remaining faithful to teaching the principles of war the Germans successfully completed their missions and brought temporary victory to Chiang's China and final victory to Franco's Falange.

Question X:

What is the most favorable size for a military mission?

It appears that the answer is an inverse proportion: the smaller the mission, the greater the mission's success. Greater benefits accrued when the advisors and technicians sent to the host country numbered under six thousand.

Outer Mongolia was reputedly conquered by two hundred or six thousand Soviet troops (depending on which version you accept). It was probably six thousand Soviet troops which repelled the White Cossack attempt to harass the Trans-Siberian Railroad; there were probably two hundred Soviet troops in Rokossovsky's military mission which accompanied the Soviet-sponsored Outer Mongolian rebels to Ulan Bator.

Early Soviet success in building the Kuomintang army was based on a mission of about one hundred. Later German success in maintaining the stability of the Chiang regime is attributed to a total of one hundred and twenty eight advisors over an eight-year period.

German involvement in Spain remained constant at six thousand advisors spread between the Condor Legion (technical advisors, pilots, and armor personnel) and teachers at the military schools. This can be contrasted with the Italian infantry of 50,000 men, whose contribution to the war was considered by some to be the conquest of the women of Seville.

Soviet involvement in Spain included technical advisors, political commissars, and the International Brigade of over 50,000 men. Their failure to Sovietize thinking and to create leftist leadership in Republican Spain points to the truth of the inverse proportion theory. The larger the number of advisors sent into a host country, the less success they had when compared to a smaller number of advisors in a similar situation. One or two hundred advisors would appear to be an optimal number of helping-country personnel.

Question XI:

How did each military mission utilize the guerrilla?

After the initial success of the Outer Mongolian guerrilla bands under Soviet tutelage, each successive mission downgraded the guerrilla role. While an officer corps was being developed, little support was given to developing small guerrilla bands working at great distances from the new army.

The Soviet-oriented political arm of the Kuomintang attempted to establish bases of operation in the major cities of

China during the years 1926 and 1927. Kuomintang Communists organized the large-city urban workers rather than build guerrilla support among peasant farmers. Counterrevolution in 1927 destroyed the Red labor unions in the large cities. These labor unions proved to be inflexible in both their areas of operation and their tactics, and were thus an easy target for destruction by the right-wing Kuomintang counterrevolutionaries. Farmers living in the southern provinces had been influenced by advancing Kuomintang armies from Canton, and it was they who actually formed the first Chinese peasant communes. Unlike Borodin, who sent his agents to build new urban unions, Bleucher marched northward from Canton and allowed his soldiers and military-political commissars to proselytize the farmers.

Stalin, in power in 1927, specifically discouraged the growth of a guerrilla base. Even after the Chinese Kuomintang counterrevolution, Stalin still spoke of continued concentration of Chinese Communist efforts against large cities. Finally, refusing to follow Stalin's advice, Mao Tse-tung and other remaining Whampoa leftists established a successful guerrilla base of operations.

German advisors in China did not develop guerrilla units, but they were constantly involved in planning the destruction of Mao Tse-tung's guerrillas. The guerrilla concept never found favor in German advice to Spanish Nationalists. Even Spanish Loyalist leaders could not see the advantage of utilizing guerrillas who were not directly under their control.

The Nationalists and Loyalists in Spain missed coutless opportunities in not setting up effective urban "fifth columns" or rural partisans. Even though guerrillas originated in Napoleonic Spain, the Spanish Civil War guerrillas never effectively harassed Loyalists or Nationalists. The concept of guerrilla utilization in Ernest Hemingway's *For Whom the Bell Tolls* distorted the actual view of guerrillas held by the Loyalist officers. Whatever feeling for the guerrillas was held by the fictional general who sent Robert Jordan on his mission was not shared by other actual Spanish Loyalist officers.

Hemingway's fictional general was based on the factual General Klèber (Bleucher?), a German-speaking Slav who headed the International Brigade. Possibly because of his interest in the guerrilla, Klèber lost favor and was replaced as leader in Spain. General A. Bayo, a Loyalist commander and later teacher of Fidel and Raoul Castro, recalled bitterly the downgrading of the guerrilla by both Loyalist and Republican politicians and Soviet political advisors. As happened in China, nonmilitary Soviet political experts had undermined the effective development of guerrilla organizations.

The Outer Mongolian attitude toward the guerrilla can best summarize the approach of the military missions to the guerrilla: when no other military force could be brought into being quickly or effectively, the guerrilla was used to achieve first stalemate and then success. However, after the Soviet-supported Mongol guerrilla bands had been victorious, the Soviet mission built a modern Mongol army that quickly forgot its guerrilla beginnings.

Question XII:

What is the value of a civilian political expert on a military mission?

When foreign civilian-political experts attempted to run and to coordinate the military-political wars, they failed. Borodin failed in Wuhan, China, in 1927 due to his lack of military background. Soviet political experts believed that the answer to Spain's problem was to use the political police (OGPU) to enforce military-political discipline and conformity. The Soviets failed again in Spain. A large native Communist party membership and a large Mongolian army with only a small male population in Outer Mongolia suggests the development of a citizen soldier adept in dealing with people in the political and military spheres.

The helping-country civilian-political expert used his skills to develop native political-military leaders and to become a military expert in the command and advisory spheres. Without an extensive background in *conventional* and *unconventional* military affairs, the political experts would fail, as happened in Spain and China.

Question XIII:

Which individuals in the helping country were chosen to lead the military missions?

Military mission assignments were serious undertakings utilized as an early proving ground for later high military office. Marshal Vasily Bleucher, who called himself General Galen at Whampoa, recorded a long list of Soviet revolutionary victories. Bleucher's experience in Russia demonstrated that if a regular army could not be developed quickly enough to combat the enemy, then a guerrilla force would be useful in developing an army and a base of operation during periods of relative weakness. In Revolutionary Russia, Bleucher led the 51st Siberian "Iron" division, the finest Red division in the field from 1918 to 1922. This 51st Division was victorious over Admiral Kolchak in the Urals and over General Deniken in the Crimea. The 51st later became guerrillas to maintain the Far Eastern Marches for Russia after 1920.

The reputed leader of the Outer Mongolian expedition was Konstantin Rokossovsky, who later became minister of defense in Poland and then deputy minister of defense in the USSR. In Spain, Marshal Rokossovsky served as Loyalist advisor, along with Ivan Konev, former first deputy minister of defense of the USSR and former head of the Warsaw Pact armies, and Rodion Y. Malinovsky, Soviet minister of defense and the World War II conqueror of Budapest, Vienna, and Mukden. In Spain these three men were so close that they became known as Martinez, Manolito, and Paulito, the Spanish three musketeers. Vasily Chuikov, Soviet first deputy minister of defense and the "hero of Stalingrad," was the leader of the second Soviet mission to Chiang Kai-shek in Chungking.

Bleucher built a small, full-time elite mobile army on a firm self-sufficient industrial base. Bleucher's image of an elite army was based on that of General Hans von Seeckt and Field Marshal Ludwig von Faulkenhausen, who had achieved fame in World War I. The idea of a blitzkrieg war carried on by a mobile army using tanks and planes found favor in both German panzer armies and Soviet tank and guards armies under Rokossovsky, Konev, and Malinovsky. Von Seeckt and von Faulkenhausen headed the German military mission to China from 1928 to 1936. Their ideas were also tested by air General Adolphe Galland and tank General Ritter von Thoma in the Condor Legion in Spain from 1936 to 1939.

The military mission thus was one proving ground, in the military and political spheres, for individual ability to achieve higher rank in the armies of the helping countries.

Conclusion

Whether or not a military mission is graded successful appears related to the ability of the helping-country military personnel in developing self-sufficient host-country leadership. By establishing schools and by employing the graduates on the faculty of that school, a host-country leadership corps was developed. The only manpower required for a successful mission was about 100 helping-country military personnel capable of developing host-country leadership. The men of the military missions taught their pupils the principles of military science as well as the etiquette necessary for the leadership of men. The civilian-political leadership supplied by the helping country usually detracted from the military contribution of the mission because of the civilian failure in properly utilizing the helping country military as teachers of men and builders of native military leadership.

Rifles rather than heavy equipment, seminars rather than lectures, appeals to the downward mobile rather than to those already in power, and promises of future jobs rather than theoretical utopias are the simplified answers to other questions posed in this paper.

Perhaps there are different, possibly better, answers to the questions, answers more applicable to the present wars. Or perhaps there are really more questions that should be asked in order to develop the yardsticks for our present military missions.

SECTION III / MAO AND THE THREE "MAOSKETEERS": CHINA IN ADOLESCENT TURMOIL

Adolescence is a quest for an identity and a life-style. Youth's movement toward maturity is highlighted in the adolescent period by emulating meaningful figures of leadership and by successfully overcoming the challenges of life. Mao Tse-tung understood this adolescent quest for maturity, and he deliberately fashioned for China's youth the challenges that he felt would lead to the emergence of a responsible and mature generation of adults.

Mao's adolescents in the Red Guards are participants in a succession crisis. Red China's leadership is fast aging without being replenished. Mao is providing a crucible of stress and revolution to discover new leadership. In the Cultural Revolution, he reconstructs the elements by which he originally found the leadership to rule China for two generations. Rarely do Westerners appreciate Mao's optimistic belief that Mao's own image of man would submerge selfish desires. As a leader he idealizes the heroic while fearing the bureaucratic. Mao's youth are not to be bureaucrats or cogs in a monolithic state, but rather they are to be appropriate successors of Mao despite challenge and change. The Cultural Revolution is the guise by which the bureaucrats are bypassed. There is an underlying theme of the revolution that can best be described as "one for all and all for one." Understanding this will help us understand the spirit which pervaded the chain of events in the last five decades of Chinese history.

Until now, Western understanding of China's adolescent turmoil has been limited, evoking memories of Hitler Youth or bringing into question Mao's senile desires. In the 1930s Hitler trained German youth to trumpets and drums, to follow Nazi dictates without question. Hitler Youth members had the limited ideal of fulfilling their duty in the German legions of conquest and, in the end, defeat. One contrasts the efficient bureaucratic image of the Germany of that period with today's China. Scholars tell of tired old Chinese rulers with high blood pressure and apoplexy. Yet the Red Guards and other elements in China present inexplicable Eastern mysteries to Western scholars. Perhaps this is because our wise men are limited to poring over manuscripts and can learn only from the printed word about the land of China. Because of such limitations, scholars could not understand the emotion and romance of the heroes and ideals that permeate Mao's thinking. To feel as Mao feels, Westerners must return to their childhood and adolescent experiences and forgo the cynicism of their adult civilization.

Childhood taught us of heroes who strove to conquer kingdoms with invisible swords. As childhood passed, reality taught us that one could not do this alone. Adolescence provided the answer that not one but multiple heroes could band together "all for one and one for all" to accomplish that which one could not do alone. The prototype of this image is found in Alexander Dumas's *The Three Musketeers*. It is not a second childhood which Mao enjoys but rather is a re-creation of a successful period of growth in which Mao participated. This is the spirit found in the last fifty years of Chinese history that sages in "far-away towers" forget and that will now be re-created to help to understand Mao.

In 1920 China was split among various warlords involved in incessant battles. Sun Yat-sen envisioned a united China, but in order to rule China he needed an army. The Chinese considered army life a lower form of existence, as pillage, plunder, famine and disease followed the movements of armies. Sun felt that the total reeducation of army personnel was necessary to create an army which could be appreciated by the populace. This reeducation began with the creation of a "Little Red Schoolhouse" under Chiang Kai-shek at Whampoa in Canton. This modern military academy was no different from others which existed at that time in China, except that its advisors and teachers came from Russia. Two men stand out. The first is a man of mystery, known by many names. He is known to have appeared in Russia at times cloaked in a mask and in China wearing Oriental garb. In European Russia he took the name Sternberg from a Russian noble who had vanquished the Mongols; in the Urals and throughout Siberia he called himself Bleucher, after a Prussian marshal who had ended Napoleon's career; in China he came as Galen, for the foremost physician of antiquity. In China the Russia magician appears as a physician-teacher, treating the Chinese malady of disunity. His cure is to create the dedicated national army officer corps that would unify and bring peace to China. The second Russian teacher is Vasily Chuikov (pronounced like Zhukov). His fame is to come later as the defender of Stalingrad and the conqueror of Berlin.

The "Little Red Schoolhouse," or Whampoa Military Academy, attracted many pupils who would serve to free China from foreign domination and local warlords. At Whampoa Galen taught how to influence the peasantry to support the cause of popular revolution and how to win wars. Had Galen (as Bleucher) not conquered the Urals, the Crimea, all of Siberia and Outer Mongolia for the new Russia? Chinese pupils such as Mao Tse-tung, Chou En-lai, Chen Yi and Lin Piao, as well as Vietnam pupils such as Ho Chi Minh and Pham Van Dong, were all apt listeners.

In two years Sun's armies grew from hundreds to a hundred thousand. In 1926 they began the Northern March. Secret agents preceded the new armies to tell of changes to come. A new idealism was preached, which included land distribution, food for all, and peace. Principles of freedom were heralded across the land, and these ideas were followed by the new armies conquering everything from Canton to Shanghai.

Sun Yat-sen, the father of the movement, died unexpectedly

before the Northern March. Chiang Kai-shek harnessed the movement by allying himself with the new merchant class. Chiang's role was similar to that of Cardinal Richelieu, who had built a bureaucracy and an army to support a growing France three hundred years before. The widow of Sun Yat-sen broke with Chiang and found friends among other Whampoa officers who swore to uphold the new freedoms as well as the old memories of her husband. The Cardinal's Musketeers were now Chiang's Kuomintang; the widow's Musketeers became the leaders of the Red armies.

At first the two bands conquered as one. In 1927 the new Richelieu turned on the widow's followers. Her supporters, such as Chou En-lai, Chen Yi, and Lin Piao, fought back in Nanchang by raising the Red flag. Beaten, the widow's Musketeers fled to the hills. There, one who can best be described as a country bumpkin took the widow's men into his band of peasant followers. Mao played a role similar to that of D'Artagnan as he began to demonstrate the qualities of leadership which bind his followers to him. By firesides in the mountains, the lessons of Galen the physician and of Sun the heroic father of the movement were taught to new peasant recruits. Simple rules of order were formulated and memorized. Although most armies discard proper social rules of conduct, the rules in Mao's army were enforced. Mao had learned a lesson of power, for between the ruler and the ruled were the rule-makers who could challenge and change. Mao had cast forth a heroic image and an idealism which fathered new recruits in ever increasing numbers.

Chiang Kai-shek continually attempted to destroy the Maosketeers. But, instead, Mao's leadership created stronger bonds. At one point the Maosketeers' strength was almost destroyed as Chiang effectively surrounded their base of operations. They had to flee to the mountains for safety. Lin Piao led the vanguard troops through unknown parts of China as Mao followed with the main body of troops on the Long March. Feats of Red Army heroism were commonplace from 1933 to 1936. Later, even Japan's invasion of China, in 1937, could not stop the Red Army conquest of new territories.

In 1945 Japan collapsed. Lin Piao alone commanded 50,000 men in the Eighth Route Red Army. Mao sent Lin to Manchuria to proselytize the people and to destroy Kuomintang power. At first Lin fought in the mountains, while cities below remained unconquered. Lin again looked to the wisdom of the Russian teachers, learning from Rodion Malinovsky how Chuikov destroyed Russia's enemies in the cities. It was Chuikov who developed the tactics by which the 62nd Siberian Army (later to be renamed the 18th Red Guards Army) destroyed German might in Stalingrad and later in Berlin. These new tactics brought Lin victory against the cities in 1948. The Eighth Route Army troops could march south from the northernmost cities to Peking, from which they crossed giant rivers as their ranks swelled on their way to the southernmost parts of China. Chiang Kai-shek fled, leaving China to Mao.

In 1949 Mao carved China into seven military districts, assigning a faithful army general and an army to each area. Region by region they were centered in (1) Sinkiang, (2) Tibet, (3) Shanghai, (4) Canton, (5) Inner Mongolia, (6) Mukden (Manchuria), and (7) Peking. Lin Piao and his Eighth Route Red Army moved to the Pacific coastline (the fourth region) and became the Fourth Army, defending against Chiang's return from exile. Chen Yi received command over the third military region and the Third Army. Early stability seemed assured until Korea erupted in war. American might turned the North Korean armies, and the American troops then approached China. When America denied Mao's request for a fifty-mile-wide demilitarized zone in Korea, Mao unleashed the armies of Lin Piao and Chen Yi, which rapidly restored the Korean status quo.

When the Korean war ended, Mao turned to the Russian experience to restore the power of his wearied armies. Many generals asked for modern tanks and planes to combat American power. Mao's answer was to emulate Galen (Bleucher) who, in Siberia, had built from scratch a modern army and industrial base independent of European Russia. Both Siberian armies and Siberian industry proved an awesome military and economic weapon in World War II. German legions often date the turning point of battle in Russia from the time the yellow men and the Siberian-made tanks appeared on the horizon. Mao's attempt at industrialization of all autonomous military regions in 1957 is called the "Great Leap Forward."

Industrialization, used to produce self-sufficient military regions, failed when the successors of Stalin in Russia refused to provide further military and economic aid to China. Each regional general wanted to salvage the wreck of experiment and to maintain individual hegemony. Generals in regions 1, 2, 6 and 7 began to think locally first and nationally second. Like the nobility of old, the generals began to weaken the Central Government by strengthening their own bases of power. Armies 3 and 4 remained weakened from their Korean experience and from the absence of Lin Piao and Chen Yi, who were ministers in Peking. One problem for Mao became reestablishing the lost unity. Mao could have brought the independent generals to heel by civil war but, if civil war had come, Russia could have seized Sinkiang, India could have moved on Tibet, America and Russia could have split Manchuria, and Chiang Kai-shek could have seized Central China. It is not true that viable, intact armies are necessary to fight any invader. Even as Mao waited, war in Vietnam intervened and complicated matters, and Mao found that he could do little to help in Vietnam. Generals were so independent that Russian arms shipments could not be guaranteed to pass through regions 1 and 2 to Vietnam.

A second perplexing problem was the succession crisis. Mao's choice as his successor, Lin Piao, was not acceptable to the generals of other regions. Such generals saw a civilian figure as their best opportunity to maintain hegemony. Their choice was Liu Shao-chi, whom Mao refused for he blamed the bureaucracy for much of China's economic woes. Mao preferred to shunt the paper pushers aside, but he needed new recruits to fill the void in pushing China ahead. Mao's answer was to train and unleash the young to undermine the support of the new warlords and of their Peking allies. The Red Guard was thus created under the command of his comrade-in-arms Lin Piao. It was time to recall the teachings of the revolutionary Galen, time to recall the struggle of the Northern and Long Marches, and time to preserve this earlier spirit throughout China. The beginning beat sounded for the new Red armies to sally forth and for new heroes of China to arise. The confusion was deliberate. New leaders to be molded from the confusion of a land in torment would understand from experience the meanings of Mao's teachings and visions.

Mao's egoism suggested to him that from the Red Guards would emerge the new leadership. Earlier revolutionary days had found his captains raising successful, independent guerrilla bands far from the caves of Mao's territories. In their youthful exuberance, few captains had deserted his cause to promote their own. (This is unlike the Russian experience in which Stalin feared and exiled 1000 behind-the-line partisan leaders who had wrecked German logistics during World War II.) Mao inherently felt that his new revolutionaries would remain loyal to him. The new Musketeers were adolescents who proselytized, not *against* the regime, but *for* Mao. These adolescents could still emulate heroes and allow ideals to bind them together to save nations. Mao's conceit was that the new Maosketeers' belief in ideals during China's present trials would lead to China's growth. Mao's belief was that of a man who, with few soldiers around his firesides, found he could harness and predict the outcome of his struggles year by year with clarity and vision. His predictions, the works of Mao, are history. His latest ploy is once again to unleash forces to pattern history to his visions. Has Mao not found a way to take adolescent idealism and insure a potentially vibrant, growing and healthy China for decades?

Once upon a time in the poetry and prose of Western civilization there were magicians, heroes and mere mortals who, torn between forces of good and evil, opted for idealism and a search for a grail. Now referred to as fairy tales and mythology, they did carry forth descriptions by which responsible leadership could develop through challenge. Homer did not err in magnifying the movements of small bands of men in terms of gods. It is a key to growing civilizations to have, as did the Greeks and Hebrews, heroic images on which to build. It is a key to decaying civilizations to have large bureaucracies, as did Rome, secular and spiritual. Dumas's tale of Musketeers is a figurative story of a band of idealistic men who existed not only then but time and again. Few leaders have captured this heroic spirit of the quest for any significant length of time. Mao's creation of the Red Guards is just such an attempt at recapturing this experience for today's China and molding a future civilization in man's heroic image. Do we tell our young there are no more heroes? Perhaps when we no longer dream of heroes or shout "all for one and one for all," we are lost.

PART IV / SUMMER

INTRODUCTION

This part should be entitled "Ever the Optimist." The first section concentrates on the question of what the United Nations could do. In essence, what the United Nations could do is what a fine reading of the UN Charter suggests it could have done; that is, to establish a UN armed presence around the world. When history shows so few years of peace, it is perhaps not surprising to turn toward military forces to preserve peace. It suggests an extra direction to the politics of confrontation.

The second section offers a domestic solution to absorb the thousands of youths that are otherwise lost in an unfulfilling domestic scene. The vital act is to choose the institutional vehicle for change. The answer, a militia, is found in the American Constitution and endows a lost institution with new meaning, much as new wine would be poured into an old wine bottle. The answer should be viewed as a militarized peace corps, absorbing the energies of thousands without leading to the death of any.

The nature of appropriate leadership is tackled in Section III, entitled "Mao as Rex the Law Giver." This is a paean to a man who has begun the arduous task of training successors to ensure the routes he has mapped out will endure another forty years.

SECTION I / UNITED NATIONS MILITARY FORCES: A PATHWAY FOR THE FUTURE

In creating a workable United Nations force, it is necessary to have a blueprint for tying together the military and political factors that would make it possible. There is a need for defining the role that United Nations forces could play on the world scene and for demonstrating the limitations that can be placed on their use. A workable United Nations force would provide an opportunity to try new solutions where older attempts have proved futile and costly.

The United States and the Soviet Union were recently allegedly discussing stationing their troops along the Suez Canal in order to preserve a long-term peace. Two strong objections arose: first, the Third World nations feared that by assuming the role of policeman to the world the superpowers would bypass the interests of the smaller nations; and second, both the United States and the Soviet Union recognize that they can no longer afford to play the role of superpolicemen. A costly cycle of weapons and counterweapons development has existed between these superpowers for more than twenty-five years, although most of the devices which have been developed have never been used. At the SALT talks, which sought to reduce weapons expenditures, both recognised the futility of Soviet-American hostility. The additional burdens of maintaining large military forces in distant areas can only detract from the necessary economic contributions of the superpowers to their own people and to the Third World. How can we or the Soviet Union bear the burden of another Vietnam?

A United Nations force with defined roles and limitations could remedy these dilemmas. This proposal does not suggest that the United Nations forces should be large enough to overawe any moderate to major-sized power. It is a coordinated drafting of a proposal that could be put into effect now or at any future date, and would provide various types of forces to prevent conflict situations from escalating. United Nations military forces would be assigned to one of three roles: (1) purely military; (2) police action; and (3) civic action.

The purely military branch would consist of a reaction force whose function is immediate confrontation with military forces which have violated or attempted to violate national boundaries. The reaction force would establish a truce line using geographic defensive positions to stop national forces from moving in either direction. Furthermore, the reaction force would be available to stop extensive rioting in major cities. Since these riots usually last about three days, a United Nations Reaction Force would need to establish a rapid military presence to restore order before being replaced by policing units.

The function of the police-action unit would be similar to that of the policeman who enforces the laws of his own community. The UN Police Force would act within the laws of the country to which it was deployed, and the UN policemen would be empowered to arrest those who broke the laws of the host country and to bring the violators before local magistrates. The UN police forces would also succeed the UN reaction forces in certain situations such as maintaining truce lines or small, neutral international zones around the world.

The civic-action troops would be called in to deal with problems resulting from earthquakes, hurricanes, or other disasters, both natural and man-made. Emergency civic-action units would not be called upon to rebuild cities, but rather would restore the basic functions of civic government in instances where the government had been immobilized. They would thus serve in the restoration of supplies of food, water, electricity, and fuel. The civic-action units would function in a capacity similar to the American Peace Corps, their personnel being invited to work in areas for extended periods of time.

The presence of United Nations forces could mean that each nation would be free to restructure its own military forces to handle a lesser role. A UN military-police-civic-action presence could mean a corresponding reduction in the number of troops in various countries of the world. The presence of a fourth world force would allow members of the United Nations to redefine their national policies to include the part played by the UN forces.

A close reading of the UN Charter gives the reader the impression that the imminent development of military forces was intended. In 1945 the UN was founded by nations which had successfully fought a war against the Axis powers when they had not been able to achieve world peace by diplomatic means. The founders of the UN recognized that a major failure of the League of Nations had been its inability to act militarily. In 1945 the United States proposed that each major power contribute what it was best able to donate: the United States would contribute planes, the Soviet Union infantry, etc. The Soviet Union proposed that each of the great powers should contribute equally. Later developments in Cyprus, the Congo, and other countries revealed the need for something beyond large-scale military forces per se. Natural disasters, such as those which occurred in Peru, the Philippines, and Pakistan (in 1970), have also added new dimensions to the burden which the UN could undertake. The failure of the UN to come to grips with problems similar to those which the League of Nations could not handle suggests that the UN might meet a similar fate, unless a new blueprint is unfolded. In resolving the problem of contributions of forces, it would seem that the Soviet concept of equal contributions is more in line with the meaning and purpose of the United Nations.

The development of a UN military presence could occur as follows. Each permanent member of the Security Council could contribute one paratroop reaction division stationed in its own territory. Both France and England have developed such intervention divisions; and Communist China, the United States, and Russia have large airborne contingents as well. Each major power could contribute the equipment necessary for the transferral of personnel to the areas in need. The United States could easily earmark the 82nd Airborne Division as its paratroop reaction unit. Officers of the reaction unit would then hold rank in both the national army and the UN army.

Additional forces could be supplied by shipborne marine brigades with support equipment. Five marine brigades could easily sail the seas to be dispatched to areas of local rioting or wars.

The disposition of paratroop intervention divisions or marine reaction brigades could be decided by the Security Council. In all probability, a country would come to the Security Council to request the presence of reaction forces. Otherwise, there would be the problem of Article II, Section 7 of the UN Charter, which prohibits interference in domestic affairs. Civil wars frequently have regional and international implications, as in the Nigerian-Biafran confrontation, a war which existed within national borders. The UN, however, has legitimized regional organizations so that, if a civil war occurs, the regional organization can declare a threat to international peace. The Security Council would then act on the regional body's investigative finding to dispatch reaction troops for the establishment of truce lines. If applied in the Nigerian-Biafran situation, political negotiations might have followed which would have prevented the large number of deaths from malnutrition. A second option would have been the establishment of an effective blockade against outside military assistance to the warring factions. This option alone could have limited the scale of fighting.

The use of reaction forces should be limited to ninety days, after which time other world forces would be moved into place. These reserve police units, earmarked for UN use, would be provided by all member nations. Units of regiment size would come from those countries with a population of over ten million. Nations with a population between two and ten million would contribute a battalion, while those with a population below two

152

million would place a company in reserve. The permanent members of the Security Council would thus be limited to the role of supplying the logistical needs of the reserve forces.

The reserve forces provided by other countries would also serve a role as UN police units, to be utilized in situations such as those in New Guinea in 1962 and in the Congo in 1960. Sweden and a number of other countries have committed themselves to availing the UN of police-type forces, and additional police reserves could be drawn from metropolitan police forces, such as the New York City police, the Metropolitan London police, etc. Such an idea is not as extraordinary as it might seem, for the Metropolitan London police have already been utilized in Cyprus. The police forces of any city would be allowed to join a police reserve, to be called upon by the UN in specific situations. New York or London police could be used to deal with problems in English-speaking countries, police from Bogota or Lima in Spanish-speaking countries, etc. The presence of people who have previously participated in police work in similar situations would provide a good model for effective police work. Utilization of police forces would provide a sense of deescalation of a formerly more serious situation.

The utilization of police-type forces, whether from Third World reserve forces trained in police work or from the metropolitan police forces of member nations, could be authorized only by a vote of the General Assembly. Within ninety days the General Assembly would have to determine that a situation exists which calls for the utilization of police-type forces or the continuance of military forces. Without affirmation of the General Assembly the military forces would be required to depart in ninety days, and even if they remained, they would be subject to the command of the Peacekeeping Staff of the United Nations, under direct control of the General Assembly.

Another type of police force available for UN use would be an Interpol-type UN police force. In addition to fulfilling Interpol functions, it would be located at all major naval and air stations situated near the great oceans: at Subic Bay in the Philippines, Aden, Singapore, Gibraltar, Okinawa, Guantanamo, Vladivostok, etc. The UN police force would be responsible for reconnaissance aircraft and weather stations and in time would be used to internationalize the naval bases and airports, facilitating UN mobility in transporting troops under Security Council or General Assembly directive. An active UN police force stationed in the great naval bases of the world would allow for the fueling and operation of all navies, but a naval flotilla would be able to utilize the base only for specific periods of time. During wartime, these ports would operate as places where ships could dock, claim neutrality, and have their crews flown home. It could be that as few as two hundred men per port of call would be needed for the bases, while the greater number of people working at a naval base would be of the local citizenry. The UN Police Force would be open to any nationality and would wear UN uniforms.

Civic-action units would be selected from logistics elements of the armies of member nations of the United Nations. While on active duty in their own countries, these civic-action units would be on call by the Security Council or the General Assembly, ready to be flown to natural or man-made disaster areas in crisis intervention aircraft. The coordination of civic-action units would be under a separate civic-action staff, which would also have the responsibility of raising and maintaining the UN Peace Corps.

Peace Corps groups would work to upgrade medical, educational, agricultural, and industrial services for periods of several months to two years. Peace Corps personnel would be assigned after they had completed course work and pretesting at UN schools located around the world. Many of the individuals who volunteered for the UN Peace Corps would not be used, but instead would be trained as reserve personnel. An interesting benefit of the UN Peace Corps or Civic-Action Reserve is that it would be a UN presence in a country. If war or a natural disaster were to occur, the area could be declared a UN international zone and civic-action reservists would be called up to serve. They would be directed to open up transportation routes and to supply the linguistic capabilities in the enormous supply efforts that would be carried out.

Other institutional structures within the UN could be expanded and developed to determine the course of UN activities. At present a military staff committee exists under the Security Council. A Police Force Staff could be established under the General Assembly, and the Civic-Action Force Staff would be responsive to both major UN agencies. A separate body would also exist to provide the funding for the activities of the forces, allocating funds both for the year and on an emergency basis. A corporate structure with voting power based on manpower or monetary contributions could be created, with no country possessing more than 10 percent of the total votes. The corporate nation stockholders would then determine future funding by a 60 percent vote. If this organization voted not to refinance an operation already in existence, the UN forces would have to be withdrawn. This would allow for the system of checks and balances to operate on the staff-level committees and on the Security Council. Further, if one country withdrew its troops and money from the UN forces, the financing committee would then allow other United Nations members to take up the slack in money and manpower. The financing corporate institution would hopefully be more responsive to the General Assembly and could raise revenue outside the UN budget.

A peacekeeping academy could be another institution to be established. All crisis-intervention officers to be used in any of the three units of the UN force would be assigned to the academy for this training and for their specific UN officer appointments. At present no such institution exists. Training in the Peace Academy could include conflict resolution, the philosophy of peacekeeping, and the delineation of responsibilities of various officers. In addition, mail-order courses could be carried on with assigned UN personnel around the world.

If it had existed earlier, the UN force could have allowed for the utilization of the great generals after World War II. Such men as Marshal Zhukov (Russia), Gen. Eisenhower (America), Gen. Montgomery (Britain), and Gen. De Gaulle (France) might have played a decisive role in world peacekeeping. It is interesting to note that none of these generals used their later positions of national power for war. In such areas as Korea, Algeria, India,

155

Palestine, and Indochina, these great men advised against war or its continuance. Such generals are still available for leadership roles at the present time: Marshal Chuikov of Stalingrad and Berlin fame and General James Gavin of Normandy are but two who come to mind. The generals would be attached to the Military Staff Committee. Each of the five permanent members of the Security Council would appoint one chief of staff for either personnel, operations, intelligence, education, or logistics. On a four-month rotating basis the chiefs of staff would each serve as overall chief of staff. The Military Staff Committee chief of staff under Article 40 of the UN Charter has been given the privilege of commanding the troops in the field. Similar staffs for the police units and civic-action units could be chosen from outside the great powers and would become primary staffs for operations after a ninety-day period, unless the General Assembly voted to allow the Military Staff to continue its overall control of a deteriorating situation.

To this point the discussion has dealt with the elements necessary for assembling an international force responsive to the various roles in the conflict or disaster situations which arise. None of the ideas is original; everything outlined has been suggested previously but has never been implemented nor presented in a total package. Such a structure of forces would provide an ability to fractionate a situation. When police units are assigned to a situation, it is a statement in the world's eyes that military force is unnecessary. There may be an ability to deescalate situations by employing adequate UN maneuvers and troops stratagems. In sending a civic-action unit to a disaster area, it is acknowledging that the nation has not lost its sovereignty over its own police and military forces. In sending police forces, a nation's police capabilities are augmented without challenging the extant military situation.

If a United Nations military force is created, could it lead to an army that could challenge a superpower? The answer given by history is mainly no. The heterogeneity of the army itself would present a major check to the misuse of the armies. Heterogeneous armies in the field have not won great victories. The Persian

Empire of Darius, able to launch 600,000 troops against Alexander's 35,000 Greeks, lost. The Pan-European Crusaders had difficulties against the Turks, a smaller but homogeneous force. The Austro-Hungarian Empire had a poor showing in battle for hundreds of years due to political confusion and distrust among the various minority groups under its military commands.

An example of a heterogeneous army that could fight well for a brief period was the multinational army commanded by the Duke of Wellington at Waterloo, or the crusade commanded by General Eisenhower.

Given the previously-projected levels of its forces, it would be difficult for the UN to destroy a homogeneous army 300,000 or more strong. Instead, the UN army would serve to isolate, neutralize, and allow political forces to neutralize threats to the peace of the world.

The alternatives to a UN presence include the increasing commitment of the United States to the Middle East and the Indian Ocean. Rising Russian naval might raises the question of a counterpoise of additional American naval construction costing billions of dollars. Attempts at general and complete disarmament will continue in terms of words rather than deeds. One may hope that the presence of UN forces could allow for stages of disarmament, and through interlinking operations, the growth of mutual trust among the powers. The creation of a UN force, giving it the military backing to enforce its peacekeeping role, as envisioned in 1945, would finally give the United Nations a credibility that it has sorely lacked.

SECTION II / WHAT CAN BE DONE NOW: THE NEW MILITIA

INTRODUCTION

With rhythmic regularity, American domestic progress has been stymied by periods characterized as "times which try men's souls." At such times of impasse, America has created new "safety valves," such as opening the West, or organizational structures, such as the New Deal, to overcome the problems of the day. However, no solutions seem to last forever; perhaps their effectiveness lasts about forty years. Our history is the prime example of this axiom.

The revolution and subsequent independence of the original Thirteen Colonies (1770s) were followed by sectional disagreements and "safety-valve" expansion into the lands surrounding the great rivers south to New Orleans (1810s), as well as Florida and Texas. Later, in the 1850s, the opening of the West, in the 1890s the new industrial state, and in the 1930s the New Deal, provided the practical solutions to growing pains. Today the era of the New Deal draws to a close. And, again, practical solutions are needed. A common historic thread and a reservoir of overlooked strength which provided a factor of stability for successive eras of change were the citizen soldiers, the militiamen. Perhaps their role is an anachronistic one, but I will suggest that their importance is now greater than ever as we reach toward

158

new programs to propel American growth.

The decline of the city and lack of job opportunity, poor education and poverty are symptomatic of the failure of the old politics. Exploration of this problem will be divided initially into two parts: what can be done for the city today, and what is the magnitude of the problem faced. The solution suggested in this paper is fashioned upon the image of the citizen soldier.

WHAT CAN BE DONE?

If adequate manpower were available, then I believe the following could be done on a daily basis in the city. When morning comes, community residents could assist in the movement of traffic and in the transportation of residents to jobs in surrounding areas. Experience suggests that the acclimation of the unemployed takes days, if not weeks, in their new jobs. After community residents provide morning transportation, these residents could also provide some individual follow-up to husband each new employee over the significant period of early adjustment to his job.

Other community members will set up day-care centers for working mothers, coordinating these with Head Start Programs for preschool children. Others in the community will move into the schools to act as assistant teachers through the eighth grade, to link the community to the educational process. After school, youth programs and teen centers would be staffed by community members to provide organized recreation and educational projects for the young.

Fully staffed neighborhood information centers will exist, tied to the concept of the Little City Hall. Each center will disseminate information and communicate citizen grievances more effectively. Staff members present at police or fire stations at night could continue a steady flow of community communication to civic authority. Information centers will also coordinate participation in sanitation drives and in finding and prosecuting housing violations. From these activities community members can gain an awareness of the law, which would allow them to meet typical civil legal problems and to aid neighborhood legal offices to operate more effectively in the community.

Other residents will help staff neighborhood health centers and provide paramedical public health care. They would distribute public health information as well as help correct public health violations. Also, during the day, new neighborhood entrepreneurs will receive help in generating public interest so that businesses can survive and prosper.

In the evening hours (6 P.M. to 2 A.M.), community personnel would help patrol their own neighborhoods. The patrol would offer advice and visibility to aid the police in providing safety on the streets, in the housing projects, and on the transportation system during the high-crime hours.

These are some of the responsibilities citizens can meet. The citizens I would specifically deal with are aged 15½ to 25, neighborhood residents, to be organized in a new militia. The enormity of the problems suggests the magnitude of the response required to meet these problems.

THE MAGNITUDE OF THE PROBLEM

No exact figure is known, but after World War II there was a migration of one to five million Negroes, Puerto Ricans, and other minorities from rural, agricultural areas, to the cities. In the cities, migrants' needs could not be met by any existing organizations formerly serving other minority-group migrants or by any city or state institutions. In the 1960s a federal response through OEO programs remained poorly coordinated, and even these programs were soon limited by the drying up of funds.

The migration had increased even though job opportunities decreased as businesses moved to the suburbs. The educational system broke under the strain of overcrowded classes and inadequate discipline. Soon, the migrant areas were milling with the unemployed and the untrained adolescent dropout. Economic adversity was one cause of a growing crime rate. For the migrant,

160

the lack of rewards in the city stood out against the propaganda of the "promised land." In addition, poor housing, poorer medical facilities, and alienation from the police led to further discontent. Rioting as a means of dramatizing the problems and striking out against some of the immediate irritants has pervaded city life since 1964. In addition, the riots have led to the threat of the ghetto community being able to succeed in supporting guerrilla activity against a perceived alien system.

Past performance of the federal military force and National Guard units suggests that military response will not solve ghetto problems. This is because military response is not a community-based response, and a military response implies force, which will in turn produce a counterforce. The response needed is a quasi-police function, in which the citizen is aware of both his rights and the scope of the law. Police functions are not the jurisdiction of an alien army, which knows little of local laws and customs. The goal, then, is to repattern existing institutions so that an attack on city problems can be made, utilizing the community, the peacekeeping functions of the law, and a civic response which does not destroy the ingrained values of our system. One cannot stress enough that it is not a military response but a community response which is desirable. The best response would be a civic-action approach which helps people help themselves. The civic-action approach must be distinguished from the cops-and-robbers approach which has dominated police thinking over the past hundred years.

THE PROPOSAL: THE NEW MILITIA

Small numbers of Negro youths rose to the occasion during the riots of 1966-67 by trying to "cool" the situation. They were identified by white armbands or by white hats. They later named themselves a Community Alert Patrol. In truth, they became a citizens' militia. Their strength in the past lay in their appeal to the law and to the rationale that riots were not "the way to do it." My proposal is to institutionalize this response by recruiting both

161

males and females aged 15½ and older into the militia. Recruiting will be from within the metropolitan area in which they would serve.

This idea is not new. Civic responsibility and civic unrest were areas about which the Constitution spoke directly. The citizen soldier is the basic answer of the founding fathers for overcoming domestic strife. Article I allowed Congress the power "for calling forth the militia to execute the laws of the Union, suppress insurrections, and repel invasions." Further, the Constitution provided for "organizing, arming, and disciplining the militia and for governing such part of them as may be employed in the service of the United States, reserving to the States respectively the appointment of the officers, and the authority of training the militia according to the discipline prescribed by Congress." The rights guaranteed to the citizen are further enunciated in the Bill of Rights. Article II guaranteed a well-regulated militia. Article III does allow for the quartering of troops in neighborhood homes, but only by permission of the owners.

Recognition of the militia concept was not a passing thought of the Constitutional Convention. The Convention was called during the crisis of Shays' Rebellion. In 1787 the foundations of the Union were strained as Revolutionary Army veterans seized an arsenal to enforce their demands for back pay. Citizen militia were called upon and responded by bloodlessly scattering the veteran soldiers. Even George Washington, as Convention chairman, championed the militia concept.

Certain assumptions can be read into the constitutional approach to domestic military use. The citizen soldier would be more likely to know and be supported by the community. He would also be less likely to use excessive force. Since there was no police force in 1787, it seems implicit that the functions of the citizen soldier were essentially those of the police—knowing and enforcing the laws on a federal or state level.

The Constitution is explicit in giving control of the militia to the state governor, unless the militia is federalized. Still, Congress can appropriate the necessary monies as well as define the nature of the militia's particular use in state service. Any regular army soldiers utilized in training or in leadership positions would have to be detached from federal service. In this way, the community involved could exert pressure on the governor to choose leadership that the community would find appropriate to its needs.

American experience in Vietnam shows that the Vietnamese have more than adequately defended their homes under American direction when they have raised a large local militia. The prime example of this is the use of Special Forces campsites. There, a twelve-man American team attempted to provide leadership for a hamlet of about 10,000 people. The Special Forces goal was to utilize 1,000 community residents in a hamlet militia. Of a hundred Special Forces camps which existed at any one time during the war, less than one camp fell each year.

Before one can detail the program of a new militia, it is necessary to detail the history of the militia in this country; that is, to describe its strengths and its faults and to avoid possible misinterpretations concerning its use.

THE MILITIA IN OUR HISTORY

Over the years the militia has suffered from a lack of publicity, from a lack of leadership, and from the jealousy of the growing military establishment. The absence of an adequate history of the militia as well as the aspersions cast at the militia cause one to pause and review its history as an integral part of the whole society. Today's militia is called the National Guard, as a tribute to the Marquis de Lafayette, who named the militia of the French Revolution the National Guard.

Police and military functions were invested in the citizen militiamen from the founding of the colonies. These men were on call for defense against attack from Indians and from European powers who were contending for positions in the New World. The French and Indian Wars provided the citizen soldier with experience to gain competence in leadership, so that it was militiamen who were able to conquer Louisbourg in Canada. It was in line with this development that British forces were easily driven from Concord and Lexington and were later to be surrounded in Boston by a colonial militia of 15,000 men. In 1775, the American colonies were able to call upon 200,000 armed militia to establish independence. Again and again, under experienced leadership, militias were able to serve a meritorious role. Vermont and New York militias won in the skirmishes which led to the British defeat at Saratoga. Southern militia at King's Mountain and Cowpens forced British troops into a retreat to Yorktown. Britain's problem was that she could only hold or raid cities and positions accessible by sea. Once inland, the British were harassed and defeated in the long run by militias.

In offensive actions one would have expected that the militia would not fight as well as the Continental Blues or the British Regulars. Under the stress of training and actual combat, regular soldiers learn the discipline of offensive action. Better colonial leaders such as Daniel Morgan and George Washington remembered this maxim of war, and thus used the militia sparingly in offensive actions.

Between wars the militia easily controlled insurrection and domestic strife. During the War of 1812, 500,000 militia filled the rolls and saw service. Again, British seapower chose the time and place for battle. Army historians make much of the militia defeat at Bladensburg in Maryland and the subsequent sacking of Washington. But it was the misuse of militia troops by inadequate regular army leaders which led to this failure. Only one general, Andrew Jackson, rose from the militia and learned to handle militiamen's capabilities adequately. At New Orleans General Jackson defeated a force three times larger than his. Jackson's mixture of Tennesseans, Kentuckians, Louisianians, local pirates, and a sprinkling of regulars, shooting from behind cotton bales, was able to slaughter units which Napoleon could not have defeated. Over 50 percent of the troops who went into Mexico in a successful campaign in 1848 were National Guardsmen who had specifically volunteered for the regular army.

At the beginning of the Civil War, the South was able to call over 100,000 Guardsmen; the Union could raise 300,000

Guardsmen. Union successes in Missouri, Kentucky, West Virginia, Maryland, and Delaware were due initially to state militias which remained loyal to the Union.

Post-Civil War militias were used in supporting Reconstruction, allowing the disbanding of the large national army. When the Tilden-Hayes election split the country in 1876, the presence of adequate militia to maintain law and order prevented a second civil war. Militia use in 1877 also restored peace between labor and management without recourse to federal arms.

The demise of the militia in a policing role dates from this time. First came the rise of separate police organizations in the major cities. Then came the theories of General Emory Upton which stressed a purely military role for the National Guard. Upton's experience and research were condensed in his book, *The Military Policy of the United States*, in which he condemned the poor offensive showing of the militia as a military unit and praised the model European soldier. Upton spoke of an expandable army, a chief-of-staff system, and a large standing army. Upton's narrow theories were instituted by Elihu Root, Leonard Wood, and Theodore Roosevelt in the Militia Law of 1903. Now, the concept of the citizen soldier meant nothing to those who promoted America as an imperial power. Even the success in Philippine villages of the Roosevelt administration militialike civic-action Thomasites (prototype Peace Corps personnel who had come to the Philippines on the naval troopship *George Henry Thomas*) was overlooked.

The result of Upton's work in the twentieth century was that in World Wars I and II approximately twenty divisions in the first year of war (one half of the immediately available divisions in the field) were federalized National Guard units. Perhaps Upton had seen correctly the carnage of the wars to follow when he had viewed the Civil War in his own time. Yet he had viewed the future military establishment without any feeling for the civilian role or for civic-action concepts. One may contrast Upton's views with those of George Washington and Andrew Jackson, who each had both civilian and military experience and who had recognized an appropriate militia role and invoked the militias without qualms during their Presidencies. Interestingly enough, prior to the Revolution, George Washington had declined offers of a regular British commission, preferring to remain a colonel in the colonial Virginia militia. Washington and Jackson could easily have called for a large standing army, yet both encouraged the concept of the citizen soldier. Upton saw military force as the only defense for Union and national interest; Washington and Jackson saw citizen participation as the cornerstone of the democracy. Perhaps the Presidents could recognize what Upton and Root could not, that the fine edge of the system of checks and balances included the militia.

In the 1960s the limited military role assigned to the militia left little flexibility for the National Guard. To correct this oversight the next section envisions the structure and functions of a revitalized militia.

THE BASIC NEW MILITIA STRUCTURE

Federal guidelines can delineate the various target areas which can be chosen from statistical sources. These areas, such as high crime rate, high unemployment rate, and growing school dropout rate, would become the basic recruiting and service areas for the full-time volunteer militiaman. Approximately 1,000 men would serve in the basic unit, and they could cover an area which contained a minimum population of 300,000. Massachusetts could consider three to five units in locations such as Roxbury, Dorchester, and South Boston-East Boston. Each battalion would receive the name of an historic Massachusetts unit, such as the 12th or 20th Massachusetts Volunteers, to suggest pride in their lineage and historic continuity.

Under the combined auspices of the state Education Department and the National Guard, a basic-training unit would be established at installations leased from the regular army. The state Education Department would become responsible for the overall training program, and for providing teachers for the unit. In a subordinate position, the regular army would become responsible for teaching military sciences, maintaining discipline, and providing medical and logistical care.

A minimum six-month training program would include remedial courses to upgrade basic school skills, followed by eight weeks of basic training. The aim of these remedial courses and of any other high-school-level courses such as civics and cultural history would be to qualify an individual for a twelfth-grade certificate.

The state Education Department would continue the educational program with courses in the following specialties:

(1) Teaching. A parateachers course for assistant teaching, classroom control, and for teaching adult education courses.

(2) Law. A paralegal course for assisting in a Legal Aid Office or in a neighborhood law office. Discussion in the classroom can center around Civil Law concepts such as negligence, liability, contracts, and landlord-tenant law.

(3) Medicine. A paramedical course presenting public health material and the procedures necessary to assist in social casework, in office-type medical procedures and in basic emergency medical techniques.

(4) Police Functions. A parapolice course presenting the nature of criminal law, showing the present government structures for fighting crime, and demonstrating the aspects of patrol. In this course the local police could stress the types of problems found in the local community.

(5) Leadership and Operations. A course stressing working in a community, community awareness, communication skills, and leadership qualities.

Each course would take approximately six to eight weeks. Each militiaman would have to qualify in a minimum of one skill before placement in a unit. Before placement in a community, each militiaman would receive an orientation course to feed back necessary community information.

The basic unit would be a ten-man team. Each team would contain two specialists in each field—two neighborhood information specialists, two parateachers, two paramedics, two paraadvocates, and two parapolicemen. The neighborhood information specialist would lead the team. If the team were to split in two, the other neighborhood information specialist would be leader.

Each team member would begin in the community as a private first-class and rise over the next year to a sergeant. The basic unit could be called a Red Team. Every four or five Red Teams would fall under the control of a Blue Team specializing in communication, transportation, and command. Blue Teams would call for a major and a captain as leaders, with room for eight other neighborhood information specialists who would double as communicators and drivers. Three or four Blue Teams would receive their logistic support from a White Team of 25 men forming a logistics-and-supply center. The White Teams would not be in the chain of command, but rather would fall under the staff logistics section of the command headquarters. White Teams could be filled from the military.

The battalion commander would be a colonel. Under him would be a chief of operations and a chief of staff with a staff of specialists including teachers and detached army physicians, legal officers, engineers, and signal personnel. A community-appointed inspector general as well as a staff consisting of adjutant general (G-1), intelligence (G-2), operations (G-3), and logistics (G-4) would back up the colonel. Civilian recruiting would be available to provide secretarial and administrative staffing (refer to charts 1 and 2).

Volunteer service would be set at two years minimum. Pay and rank would be equivalent to federal standards. In addition, each militiaman could receive GI benefits, determined by length of service, to apply to future schooling. No volunteer could be federalized until age 18. Yet, the same individual could take any army-given courses in any part of the country as part of the militia experience. After finishing two years of militia service he could continue in the militia, join the regular army with credit for service, or move on to college.

No community tour would be longer than four years. At that time the individual could choose a year of federal service or full-time police work. Later, those who chose to do so could rotate back into the militia. The skills of these community specialists, when better known, could find increasing use in federal service in cross-cultural areas.

Between the colonel, the governor, and the community

would have to exist a directory-general of community members who would have a veto over the colonel's actions, as well as a recommending function to the governor. Another important communication link would be a permanent directory-general assigned to the Pentagon to approve and recommend changes in the new Militia Act.

This portion of the paper has stressed the benefits of service, individual militia training, and the outline of the units. The next discussion is of the interactions between the community and the militia.

CHART II

OUTLINE OF BASIC STRUCTURE: Table of Organization

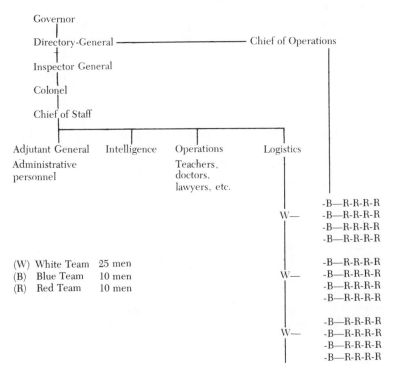

CHART III
Approximate Staffing

(W)	White Team	25	total—	75
(B)	Blue Team	10	total—	120
(R)	Red Team	10	total—	480
				675
	Command Unit 150 (excluding White Teams)			150
				825
			in training	175
			total—	1,000

THE MILITIA IN THE COMMUNITY:
CONTROL AND UTILIZATION

Constitutionally, the appointment of all officers would rest in the hands of the governor to maintain appropriate federal-state relationships. Community control could be maintained by instituting a civilian board, called a Directory-General, which would stand in the chain of command between the governor and the militia colonel. The Directory-General would nominate one or more individuals for any officer rank, to be approved finally by the chief executive of the state. Initially, the Directory-General would consist of seven members: one representative from the governor's office, one from the mayor's office, one from the police commissioner's office, and four representatives elected by the community. The power of the Directory-General would be to approve or veto by a two-thirds vote any policies or actions undertaken by the colonel, finally submitting their decision to the governor for approval.

Operations by the militia in the community would be flexible. Initial deployment would be subject to the recommendations and goals as set forth in plans approved by the Directory-General, the colonel, and the governor. Initial planning could divide police and community-action functions equally. Unless emergency situations arise, no more than 50 percent of militia time would be spent on police functions. Daytime utilization may find a Blue Team operating a neighborhood information center, while Red Teams operate day-care centers, arrange transportation

170

and job interviews, act as assistant teachers in school, and help the legal and medical facilities in the community. Blue Team leadership can request from the White Teams reserve manpower to work on afternoon youth projects and on public health measures such as massive cleanup campaigns or towing away cars. Militia support can provide aid to youth projects providing community activity for all. Further utilization of militiamen will consist of aiding or running afternoon education centers and libraries, teenage workshops and coffee houses, and adult-education programs.

The militia can mobilize the geriatric population to join and attend Golden Age clubs. A meal on wheels program could also reach out to the older population. Projects to reach out to the adult population would provide the manpower to spot housing violations and to work with city functionaries to bring violators to court.

Female militia members would be useful in many of the above projects. It may be found that females work better with specific age and sex groupings.

Patrol and police functions in the community would be concentrated around a 6 P.M. to 2 A.M. schedule. Each Red Team assigned to patrol would be joined by two policemen, whether city police, housing police, or transportation police. While a Blue Team would operate a Blue Team headquarters or use a police station, both the Blue and Red Teams would fall under police control. Patrol functions would stress a high degree of visibility. Patrol of housing projects would find Blue and Red Team members living in the housing project for a period of time. In the housing project, paramedics could staff satellite night emergency-care units, along with a detached army physician. The weapons of a patrol of housing projects would find Blue and Red Team members and tear gas or Mace.

In time, community leaders, expressing themselves through the Directory-General, could find that educational assistance should be the prime concern of the unit. Such directives could allow the colonel to assign to the schools, full-time, one or more Blue Teams and their Red Teams. Each Red Team would now be directed by the parateacher member of the team. The Blue Team leader would receive the position of an assistant principal in the school, reporting directly to the principal and in direct charge of the militiamen in the school. The presence of minority-group members in authoritarian roles would have significant positive effects on the young of the community.

If safety in the streets were the concern of the community, then the community could use a Blue Team during the day as a clearing house for citizen information to be relayed to the police without identifying the sources of information. Blue Team members could present lectures in burglary prevention and thus form small citizen groups to open up communication with the police, overcoming the problems of apathy.

As the militiamen would be members of the community, they would be encouraged to spend their free time voluntarily helping businesses and gaining further education. They could help new businesses by providing publicity and free aid to the businessmen in overcoming the initial heavy expenses. The state Education Department would also have educational classes for the militia and the community. These could be in cultural history, social sciences, or science. Some courses would be job training courses which would be sponsored by local labor unions.

The cornerstone of participation of a militia would be its flexibility. This section has provided only a sprinkling of the various types of involvement the militia could have in a community.

THE MILITIA: POTENTIAL PROBLEMS AND OBJECTIONS

Sources of potential problems in raising a militia relate to the individuals recruited; to the nature of the control mechanisms, whether federal, state, or community; to the problem of the separation of functions; to the nature of the funding; and to the question of whether the militia would alleviate any of the problems of crime and disorder in our cities.

(1) The Individual Recruited

Possible objections to an individual militiaman relate to his age, to his recruitment standards, and to his discipline. Another problem would be what the program offers the recruit.

The Constitution did not set any requirements for the proper age for voting or for army service. Each state has been free to choose its own standards. Federal army standards have allowed 17-year-olds to volunteer. I suggest that 15½ be the minimum age of recruitment. The basis for choosing this age is that our present educational system loses control over the majority of potential dropouts at this point. In fact, in most states there is no requirement to attend school at age 16. A strong argument for recruiting at this age comes from United States experience with Viet Cong troops in Vietnam.

The militia will accept only volunteers who have parental consent. There would be no draft. Organizations which begin and continue on a volunteer basis have the best chance of success. The regular army finds that its best units have been all-volunteer units. An example is Special Forces.

Many individuals volunteering may have had a previous encounter with the law. Juveniles who are convicted felons could possibly be approved by the office of the Directory-General.

In the militia the individual would be subject, first, to the laws of that community and state, and second, to federal law. Severe disciplinary problems could be handled first by psychiatric evaluation, and then any recommendation for release from militia service would be passed upon by the Directory-General. Individual militiamen would also be helped with their problems by the unit inspector general, his state representatives, or the governor.

The promise of the militia to the individual is the opportunity for him to gain a twelfth-grade certificate and the benefits of the GI Bill, to be used in college or in a vocational specialty. He would also have the option, while in militia service, to attend any army school of his choice. Above all, when he finished his two years of minimum service, he would have gained an understanding of his community and a pride in its accomplishments.

(2) Problems of Control

The federal government would draw up the broad outlines of the requirements of the program. Initially a separate department for the militia within the National Guard would be created in the Pentagon. Then, an overall Directory-General would be established to maintain communication, report directly to the President, and act as liaison for the state units in congressional hearings. Members of the Federal Directory-General would hold rank as high as Brevet General Officer. Their appointments would come from the President on the basis of recommendations from the state governors. These high-ranking officers should be educators, social scientists, lawyers, physicians. A second tier of officers would be police and military experts. Personnel of the stature of Kenneth Clark, Earl Warren or Arthur Goldberg would be prime candidates for the Directory-General. The Directory-General would draw up budget requests, maintain standards for the decentralized units, and hold the power of investigation.

The operation would rest with the state governor, who would be the commander in chief of the state unit. His power could be overridden only through electoral process or by federal law. The community would, however, exert a great deal of influence, and the community would also have the option of utilizing the referendum to disband the program. Community acceptance of the envisioned police civic-action program would require continuing approval.

It should be noted that within the program the regular army would have no command function. This would continue the distinction between a military attitude and that of the citizen soldier. Certainly, enlisted troops would be detached for service in the battalion headquarters or on the White Team. However, for an officer to hold state officer rank, he would have to be approved by the community. In the past, military civic-action programs have succeeded only when figures such as Douglas MacArthur and Leonard Wood in Japan and the Philippines have worked in a civilian rather than a military capacity.

Police control of militia activities should be limited to joint patrols. Should the mayor request patrol functions outside the community, these patrol activities would fall under the control of the responsible police captain. Any other city agency requesting Red or Blue Team aid would filter its direction through the responsible Blue Team leader.

At all times control would remain with the citizens through elections. Success of the program would depend on the respect and pride that could be generated within the community. Although white citizens might look askance at raising a minority-group militia, initial programs would seek to match predominantly white target areas with nonwhite areas to overcome prejudices.

(3) Separating Military, Police, and Civic-action Functions

An important problem would be the choice of attitude to be impressed on the militia. A civic-action mentality would suggest helping people to help themselves; a police mentality would suggest a safety-first approach; and a military mentality would suggest force. The promotion of a civic-action function as primary would mean a continuing downgrading of the other militia phases. The military phase would begin and end with basic training. Basic training would be used to meet National Guard requirements as well as to provide an initial hurdle for trainees to overcome. This would become the common melting pot, providing stronger bonds among militiamen. No further required military-type training would take place during the first two years of service. Police functions such as arresting criminals or stopping crimes would be left to the police. The militia would function as an organization to help the police perform community activities that police cannot perform adequately today. These services include providing police presence in the streets and maintaining strong community contacts. Militiamen would be taught that they need not catch criminals nor write traffic tickets. By limiting patrol functions to 6 P.M. to 2 A.M., and by allowing no individuals to serve more than 50 percent of their time on patrol, it is hoped that a police mentality could be avoided.

Previously, a civic-action approach has been applied to underdeveloped areas. Since the militiamen would now be speaking the same language and having the same goals as the population, this approach would appear more promising.

The proposed six months educational program would be needed to promote the civic-action approach. Leadership would be chosen having some qualifications in a civic-action approach, thus reinforcing it in the community.

(4) The Cost

Program financing would be a federal responsibility. Pay scales and extra allowances such as housing and travel would be equivalent to regular army pay scales. Each 1,000-man unit plus logistical support would cost about $15,000,000 yearly (comparable regular army unit cost is $55,000,000). The estimate for the number of units per city would be one unit per 300,000 population. Thus, Boston, with over 600,000 individuals, could request two units.

(5) Crime, Violence, and the Program's Promise

The program would offer immediate employment to the community population. By recruiting 15½- to 18-year-olds, the age group which currently has the least opportunity for employment would become the target employables. This is also the age group which commits the most crimes today. These young people would thus be presented with the possibility of visible rewards in their own communities. This would present another outlet for gaining peer-group approval rather than having to seek approval through vandalism.

The success of the program would be in supplying the militia spirit to the subcultures of the neighborhood. The most dangerous threat to the fabric of our society is guerrilla warfare in the streets. The militia would offer an opportunity to cut the potential guerrilla from his source of encouragement—the community. Isolated incidents could more easily be spotted and localized. Potentially explosive situations which in the past have led to riots could now be handled by the immediate presence of the militia. In such situations the militia would act as a mediating agent, if not as a "coolant."

CONCLUSION

The first war on poverty was fought without an army. It did not enlist in the fight those whom it attempted to help. The second war on poverty, by utilizing a militia, would attempt to reach the community and to meet community needs. The second war would also utilize education to a greater extent. In fact, during the first war, no educational institution trained any of the warriors.

The militia is our historic reservoir by which past challenges to domestic and international security have been met successfully. In each era the militia has adjusted its purpose to meet the needs of the time. Today's challenge is to meet the civic needs and to restore the lost sense of community. Properly infusing these ideals into the militia would produce an organization necessary for the struggle ahead.

SECTION III / MAO AS REX THE LAWGIVER

Once before I had turned to researching the problems of China and had focused specifically on the problem of succession. On April 28, 1963, the *New York Times Magazine* printed an article which suggested that the successor to Mao Tse-tung was to be Lin Shao-chi, Chou En-lai, or Teng Hsiao-p'ing. In an unpublished letter to the *New York Times* on April 28, 1963, I wrote:

It is with the line of succession to Mao Tse-tung that I find myself in more disagreement. There is in Peking a group of Chinese marshals and generals who originally raised the flag of the Communist revolt against Chiang Kai-shek in Nanchang in 1927. These soldiers—Lin Piao, Chu Teh, Chen Yi, and Chou En-lai—are a band of officers who have supplied the military thought and leadership to the Chinese Red Army since 1927, a source of power that remains under their control at the present. As the years have progressed they have risen to head the Ministry of Defense, the Red Army, the Foreign Ministry, and the Premiership of the Republic. For in China, as well as in the Soviet Union, the royal road to power is through association with and control of the military, a point not well appreciated as yet by many analysts of the Communist World. From the above list of officers, Chu Teh may be eliminated as a successor on the basis of his age. Chou En-lai's future success lies in his support by Lin Piao and Chen Yi, as he is the furthest of the three from the source of power, the military. In fact my information is that the most respected of this band of officers, as well as politicians, is

178

Lin Piao. On the basis of the above reasons, my three pictures (choices) would show Lin Piao, Chen Yi, and Chou En-lai.

In 1966 Lin Piao was recognized as the heir apparent to Mao Tse-tung.

My interest in China's future was reawakened when the Red Guards became more and more enigmatic to Western writers. "Mao and the Three Maosketeers" is a rethinking and pulling together of ideas on Mao and his revolution.

In his childhood Mao was influenced by a book called *All Men Are Brothers*. The book appears to be the Chinese version of the Three Musketeers. *All Men Are Brothers* is a tale of heroic bandits in revolt against the corruption and the bureaucracy of an older Chinese kingdom. They fought from a mountain lair. In Mao's first military campaign he was asked what should be done in battle. He suggested that the soldiers should act like the heroes in *All Men Are Brothers* and retreat to a mountain hideout.

For forty years Mao has been a ruler or rulemaker in China. In 1927 he headed an organization containing ten million peasant members; in 1969 he headed a China of 750 million people. As the acknowledged living theoretician of revolution, Mao should have many ideas on the nature and creation of law and its interactions with man.

Lon Fuller, in his book *Morality of the Law*, recognized that charismatic rulers do arise. By utilizing the basic theme of "all for one and one for all," these rulers are able to create an atmosphere in which new modes of rules for their followers are easily acceptable. But Professor Fuller treats these figures as aberrations, perhaps because, on first glance, the Mao-type figure appears to be a positivistic law giver; that is, the law is, in effect, what Mao says it is.

This may be a gross oversimplification, but it finds support in the few books on China which have headings on law or jurisprudence in their indices. Extensive reading, however, brings out some interesting points on the relationship of Mao and the law. On the Long March to Yennan, the most important object preserved en route was a black iron box containing the Organic Constitution (1931) and Laws of the Soviet Regions. Mao and every important Communist figure would, in rotation, constantly guard the iron box. Mao and his followers gave the impression of their subordination to principle and to law.

Mao's Soviet was created in 1927, although the constitution was not published until 1931. When Mao exerted control over China in 1949, he waited until 1954 to publish a new Chinese constitution. Initially Mao set up broad principles and guidelines. He then waited four or five years before codifying the new rules. In the interim he watched the nature of the interactions of the people under those guidelines and, when answers began to emerge, he codified the new interactions into law. Mao first learned this method of lawgiving in 1926 in Hunan Province. He suggested to the provincial people that, under the principles of the Kuomintang Revolution, the estates of large landlords should be given to all the poor peasants. Mao then watched as people's courts arose to distribute the land. He saw the courts develop a rationale for removing the landlord from his property. He also saw the people's courts make the landlord, through self-criticism and through endless cross examination, repudiate his past actions. Today we call this process "brainwashing."

In 1926 Mao had seen what the people could do. He set forth the patterns in writing for other people's courts to adopt. A procedural aspect of Mao's methodology is that he limits initial experimentation to a small area before promoting the experiment on a large scale. Unnoticed in the reporting of the turmoil created by the Red Guards is the fact that they were first limited to the largest cities. They were first utilized in Peking and later spread to other urban areas, but they have been kept out of communes in the countryside.

Final adoption of the new laws appears to follow the customs which have sprung up in the interactions of the people over time—in effect, the customary laws. The rules that arise in the interactions of the people using the broad guidelines are then viewed and refined by the lawmakers. This process is the probable basis of the phrase "socialist legality" which is often bandied about in Communist writings. From this attitude comes the assumption that the laws have emanated from the people. In effect, Mao appears to validate the latest customs of the people, but these are within the broad guidelines which Mao himself has enunciated.

In the choice between a morality of aspiration and a morality of duty, "Mao and the Three Maosketeers" makes clear that Mao has chosen a morality of aspiration. He would express this as a contrast between an heroic civilization and a bureaucratic civilization. His actions suggest that the rulemaker has an additional role to play in maintaining the morality of aspiration. This role is to keep before the people a progressive series of challenges to maintain a sense of "permanent revolution" until all goals are realized.

Mao is constantly reaching out to use all the energies of man in his revolution. The mentality of the modern scientist and the government welfare planner is therefore shunned when their planning does not effect a full utilization of man's strengths. Mao would agree with Professor Fuller that "the morality of aspiration has to do with our efforts to make the best use of our short lives."

An examination of Mao's career shows him to be a strong exponent of the characteristics of the internal morality of the law, procedures for governing human conduct under substantive rules. Professor Fuller has outlined the eight basic procedural rules:

(1) The rules must be made known (publicity)

From the first poster Mao hung on his classroom wall to the posters of the Red Guards, Mao has clearly tried to publicize the guidelines and the rules of conduct. Few authority figures have been as prolific in writing the rules necessary to guide the conduct of man. Very few of Mao's writings are known to be unpublished, and these few have been his poems. It is very unlikely that in 100 years there would be unearthed a book of *Secret Instructions*, as there was for Frederick the Great about 140 years after his death. Mao has achieved his publicity through poems, newspaper editorials, pamphlets, articles, and extensive interviews. Many journalists have spent hours interviewing Mao, and these interviews have also been widely publicized. Literacy campaigns have swept the country. Many areas of China today boast 100 percent literacy. This, too, has helped the dissemination of the works of Mao and, therefore, the policies of Communist China.

(2) There must be general rules

In 1949 Mao promulgated a principle of socialist legality, stating that the rules must be general enough to be understood by the average individual. In creating rules for the army, Mao developed short poems to be committed to memory. These mnemonic devices to facilitate learning are composed of eight phrases and are still learned by every new Red Army soldier. In the same manner, battle tactics were committed to memory through short phrases. This paper has already described the experimental waiting necessary prior to refinement and promulgation of general rules of conduct.

(3) The rules must be reasonably clear

The *Red Book* of Chairman Mao's sayings is the most reprinted book in history, perhaps surpassing the Bible in circulation. Yet these sayings are a product of constant revision and explanation to achieve clarity. The endless popular Chinese discussions of Mao's thoughts and self-criticism sessions are basically aimed at clarifying these thoughts.

(4) The laws should not be contradictory

Mao has written works specifically on resolving contradictions. He suggests that many contradictions are resolved by an individual placing himself in the historic time span of Communist development. Mao's China in 1927 was a feudalistic society; Mao's China in 1947 was a bourgeois society. The year 1954 saw the beginning of socialism on a large scale. The goal, of course, is to attain communism. In each transitional stage, contradictions develop. The resolution is to place oneself in the proper historic period to appreciate the guidelines from which the appropriate rules of conduct are adopted.

(5) The laws should not require the impossible or unreasonable

One thesis of this paper is that Mao has adopted the customary laws of conduct as developed by the people. This suggests that Mao has avoided the many laws which would have proved unreasonable. Mao's tenure as ruler and the lack of organized resistance to his leadership suggest that the laws in practice are eminently workable.

Mao recognized that the movement from bourgeois legality to socialist legality would leave a number of bourgeois individuals who would find it difficult to adapt to the new legality. Mao's answer was rather unusual to Western ears. In 1949 he deprived this group of their voting rights as well as other legal status. After the re-education campaigns and after the acceptance of the new rules by the bourgeois, these groups were again accepted into legal status. Mao's answer to the problem of impossibility of performance is that, if persons cannot conform to the law, they are placed outside the law until they have been re-educated.

(6) The laws must not be retroactive

Mao could have pointed to the laws of the First Soviet promulgated in 1931, and he could have stated that as each new area came under his control the people had the old guidelines on which to fall back. But Mao's approach was to recognize that the people of a newly conquered area would at first not accept the

Communist program wholeheartedly. Mao's practice of holding off the promulgation of laws for a few years allowed the new relationships to develop themselves before principles of legality were established.

(7) There should be a congruence between legal rules and the administration of the laws

Large-scale rectification campaigns suggest that the administrators and the rules are constantly provoked into interactions. For administrators, this has meant returning to the fields and factories, and for military officers, returning to the ranks for short periods of time. By exposing the administrator to the conditions he is administering, potential incompatibilities are forestalled or rectified. The scope of the rectification program reveals the importance that Mao places on bringing the rules in line with the conditions the rulers administer.

(8) The laws should be constant through time

Mao's effort is directed toward promoting the permanence and the infallibility of the broad principles of his program. The deification of Mao can be more appropriately labeled the deification of Mao's thought which, through inculcation in the young, attempts to achieve permanence over time.

Mao has often gone into seclusion for long periods and has then emerged to lead mass campaigns until the people can accept the principles on objective and impersonal terms. Mao's seclusion suggests to the people an image not unlike the biblical figures who went into the wilderness or to the mountains to meditate. Mao's thoughts, when presented to the populace, are then rethought or acted upon by all.

These Maoist truths are presented as historic principles which by themselves will remain stable through time. It follows from this that the laws promulgated under these historic principles will also enjoy some of this stability.

Some people feel that the eight principles of legality were based on a ninth principle of permanent stable government. Mao Tse-tung would reject a sense of stable government in this scheme of legality. First, Mao would feel that the success of his system depends upon maintaining a morality of aspiration. To do this, there is a need for a constant rededication to principle or, in Mao's terms, for a permanent revolution. Mao's legacy to his successors is the need for a constant rededication to the utilization of all of man's energies. Second, Mao would suggest that by substituting stable, broad guidelines and principles, there would be little need for the outward form of a stable government. In fact, Mao believes that in his Communist utopia his government would wither away. This would explain his lack of concern for the outward turmoil of the present Chinese government as it rededicates itself to principle. It would also follow that removing party and government officials is of little consequence in the maintenance of a sense of legality.

If Mao were Rex the Lawgiver he would have created for the new legality a revolutionary fervor within the population by first presenting broad principles and guidelines to the people. Rex would then have promoted people's courts to develop the laws. He would have chosen those rules that seemed to work best by studying the interactions of the new laws with the population. In this way Rex would then have made the populace feel that they had developed the law. Rex would have waited a few years before implementing his new codes.

In addition, Rex would have maintained a constant outflow of writing on the broad principles to which he subscribed. In this way, he would have indicated a subordination to these principles. Also, Rex would have attempted to create the type of psychological experiences that would reinforce the principles to which he subscribed. The challenge of these experiences would lead to a renewal of a common understanding of the nature of his external legal system. Such psychological manipulation would then become a repetitive experience in Rex's kingdom. These were some of the means utilized by Mao, as a lawgiver, in moving China into the phase of rapid growth necessary to develop a modern nation.

Mao places in perspective the limits of the law in the context of social revolution. The Red Guards are the force from which Mao is to find the new leadership for a growing China. He takes a psychological force such as adolescent turmoil and allows this force to become an effective support for his attempt to institutionalize permanent revolution.

Some of the difficulty in understanding Mao is his use of customary law. Mao circumvents immediately effecting new positivistic-type laws in China by appealing to a morality of aspiration, through which the people's courts develop the new rules of law. In addition, Mao uses subordination to principle and an historic scope interacting with a fidelity to the internal morality of the law to produce a context in which China can rapidly grow. Mao hopes this growth, which utilizes all of man's energies, will lead China into a leading position as a world power and will break the feudalistic bonds which have kept China subordinate to Western cultures in importance.

TEMPORARY CONCLUSIONS—1970

(THE CLIENT IN A STAGE OF DEPRESSION)

THE AMERICAN FALL, THE RUSSIAN WINTER, THE CHINESE SPRING—AND SUMMER

American foreign policy, which is hinged on a 1940 ideal, is rushing toward bankruptcy. I do not expect a realignment of foreign-policy goals until 1980. Instead, I watched Henry Kissinger and Richard Nixon acting as Prince Metternich and Emperor Franz Joseph legitimizing a coalition of superpowers. In 1970, history left us searching for solutions to American domestic problems. Almost forty years of a New Deal left a nation without solutions to the problems which the New Deal created. The search for solutions to such problems as those of the small businessman, economic growth, welfare, education, law and order, and medical-care costs is more necessary now since, by successfully solving domestic problems, we could once again face the international scene with suggestions for fundamental changes. As no domestic solutions are evident on the horizon, I fear that I am seeing the American Fall. Where are the Thomasites of yesteryear?

The Russian Winter, after the stability provided by the Siberian Army, reflects the passing of the heirs of Bleucher. Instead, with Malinovsky's death and the Czechoslovakian invasion of 1968, old harsh elements gained ascendency in Russia. Marshal Konev turned his back on a defensive posture, promoting the interests of the navy and air force to the detriment of the infantry soldiers. Perhaps, as former governor general of Czechoslovakia, he could not turn his back on friends who were being displaced in Prague. Other army chiefs refused to invade. Instead, Stalinist generals were brought out of obscurity to lead the invasion. A countercoup with an attempt on the life of Brezhnev led to the death of over 100 generals in 1968, as they had failed to protect the influence of Bleucher on the Soviet military. A more belligerent and aggressive Soviet navy and air force have chosen to flex their muscles in Egypt and Vietnam. Bleucherites, perhaps, are in a deep freeze, hopefully to be later thawed.

The Chinese Spring reflects the ability of Mao Tse-tung after a forty-year hiatus to reinculcate a new young leadership to guide his revolution for another forty years. It is the Chinese vitality and youthful leadership which will maintain the Chinese momentum in the near future.

Summer on the world scene reflects to me the hope that the United Nations, although scorned by many, has the seeds of a brighter future for the world.

I have learned through my travels not to be an alarmist but rather to allow the tides around us to be recognized and studied. The questions of leadership, cultural change and the dynamics of successful civilizations have always been with us. Tools for understanding these phenomena are within the scope of a historian, but it is to other fields that I turn in my middle years to find answers after having found some of the appropriate questions.